Managing God's Organization
The Catholic Church in Society

Research for Business Decisions, No. 79

Richard N. Farmer, Series Editor

Professor of International Business
Indiana University

Other Titles in This Series

Managing God's Organization
The Catholic Church in Society

by
Scott R. Safranski

UMI RESEARCH PRESS
Ann Arbor, Michigan

Produced and distributed by
UMI Research Press
an imprint of
University Microfilms International
A Xerox Information Resources Company
Ann Arbor, Michigan 48106

Library of Congress Cataloging in Publication Data

Safranski, Scott R. (Scott Richard), 1951-
Managing God's organization.

(Research for business decisions ; no. 79)
"A revision of author's Ph.D. thesis, Indiana
University, 1983"—T.p. verso.
Bibliography: p.
Includes index.
1. Catholic Church—United States. 2. Sociology,
Christian (Catholic) 3. Church management. I. Title.
II. Series.
BX1406.2.S23 1985   262'.0273   85-16540
ISBN 0-8357-1669-4 (alk. paper)

To Dorothy, Sally, and Kent

Contents

Figures and Tables

Preface

With over 700 million members, the Roman Catholic church is a large multinational enterprise with personnel and resources in virtually every part of the globe. It is a vast bureaucracy which has survived frequent hostility through nearly two millennia of internal and external change. It has acted as a mediator for governments and its pronouncements on economics and politics remain the subject of much interest and debate.

Clearly religious organizations, such as the Catholic church, are influential actors in the business and economic environments. Through their pronouncements on politics and economics, activities as purchasers of goods and services, roles as teachers, and positions as members of numerous communities, large religious organizations have impact reaching well beyond the lives of their immediate members. Nevertheless, these important organizations are little understood beyond the religious community itself.

In the following pages the Roman Catholic church is studied from an organizational, rather than a theological, perspective. The focus is the interaction of units, at various levels of the church's hierarchy, with groups outside the church. This focus facilitates the identification of important external groups and organizations. Church organization and management processes are then studied in terms of adaptations made in an effort to assure cooperation and stable relationships with important internal and external interest groups and resource suppliers.

It is hoped that this book, a management study, will improve understanding of the church as a social and political organization. Information regarding the management processes of this huge organization should be useful to managers of religious institutions, managers who deal with them, and other institutional managers who might benefit from additional management knowledge in general.

Study of such a complex organization would not be possible without the cooperation and assistance of many others. I am most grateful to all those in the Roman Catholic church who spent valuable time answering questions and providing information. In particular I would like to thank the Archbishop and many employees of the Archdiocese of Indianapolis and the Indiana Catholic Conference. All those contacted in these church units went out of their way to be helpful and to make this researcher's job much more pleasant. My respect for the Catholic church and its representatives has been enhanced considerably as a result of my contacts with these dedicated people.

I would also like to thank Professors Richard N. Farmer, George W. Wilson, Janet P. Near, and Mary Jo Weaver who, as my research advisers, contributed significantly to this study. I am indebted to Dr. Ik-Whan Kwon and Saint Louis University for the support to finish this book in timely fashion. My thanks also to my typist, Ms. Kelly Cartwright. She patiently accepted revision upon revision while taking my own deadlines to heart in spite of concurrent commitments to many others.

Finally, I would like to thank my wife, Sally, for her very patient and unfailing support. Much of her leisure time was used to proofread the manuscript and to set up most of the tables and figures. More of her time was sacrificed in taking on extra household responsibilities to allow me more time to devote to this project. She remained confident during my own periods of doubt and put up with her husband's incessant rambling about research which could not have been as interesting to her. For all this, and more, I am most grateful.

The contributions of all of these people, and certainly many others who will go unmentioned, have added considerably to the quality of this book. Any errors or inadequacies are, of course, entirely my own.

1

The Economic and Political Influence of Religion

*... those who say that religion has nothing to do with politics
do not know what religion means.*

—Mahatma Gandhi

*The Christian has the duty to take part in the organization and
life of political society.*

—Pope Paul VI

If asked about the influence of religious factors on their markets or
management techniques, most executives would probably suggest that they
have little impact, if any (and most would probably think the question a bit
odd). The vast majority of managers and business scholars pay little attention
to religious groups except, possibly, as part of their own traditional worship
habits. As a result very little study of the impact of religion on the economic
sector has been done.

Nevertheless, recent events testify to the fact that religious sects and their
leaders make frequently successful efforts at exerting influence on economic
and political events. Iran, India, Egypt, Israel, Poland, Northern Ireland,
Lebanon, and Saudi Arabia continue to make news largely as a result of
religious tensions. In the United States, political debates on abortion,
economics, and defense are led by religious groups and their hierarchies.

Some examples of major incidents in 1984 involving religious groups are
recounted in an article in the January 2, 1985, issue of the *Lutheran* magazine.
Events cited in the article include the suspension of two white Lutheran
churches in South Africa for refusing to publicly reject apartheid, a
controversy between a Lutheran pastor and his bishop over economic policies
and practices in Pennsylvania mining areas, the deportation by the Taiwanese
government of two Presbyterian missionaries considered to be subversive,

and the resistance of fundamentalist church schools in Nebraska and Maine to government controls. Fundamentalist religious groups frequently make the news regarding their views on what records, books, and magazines should be published, and publish their own performance ratings of various legislators and judges.

As will be seen shortly, these examples merely touch on the most publicized and, therefore, most obvious situations of religious influence. A large undercurrent of activities may be directed at individual business firms and many paths of influence might exist that are often not newsworthy but may ultimately be extremely important in their effects on businesses.

Religious organizations may gain power through attempts to influence the attitudes of the faithful, through rules laid down to be followed by their membership, or through overt organized political activity designed to modify the conditions in which businesses must operate. It should be kept in mind that most major religious sects are themselves multinational organizations. There are at least fifteen denominations which have a membership in the United States alone of more than one million. The Roman Catholic church, frequently used in business administration courses as an example of a successful bureaucracy, claims a world membership in excess of 700 million.[1] These organizations often own, or support in large part, schools and colleges, social organizations, and missionary and relief agencies. As multinationals these organizations are major movers of resources, people, and information. They are vast communication networks which, like any multinational business, are capable of concentrating power in a given sector of concern to the larger entity. As Berger and Neuhaus state, "Few institutions have demonstrated and continue to demonstrate perduring [enduring] power comparable to that of religion."[2]

Interviews with business people, academics, and clergy all suggest society's current naiveté with respect to the potential (or appropriate) influence of religion may stem from a misinterpretation of the First Amendment to the U.S. Constitution which states, in part, that "Congress shall make no law respecting an establishment of religion, or prohibiting the free exercise thereof." While this statement says nothing to indicate a limit on religious activity to influence the government and society, it is often referred to, certainly inaccurately, as guaranteeing the separation of church and state. This "separation" is then assumed to exist in fact even though it does not even actually exist on paper. The amendment is designed to protect religious practice from government interference and/or control. It does not seek to limit the input that religious and other groups may have in the political process.

This inaccurate perception of the environment, as any misinterpretation of reality, creates a danger that U.S. businesses will fail to respond adequately to important conditions which may represent opportunities as well as threats. Such a failure could lead to problems ranging from inadequate personnel and labor relations policies to inaccuracies in anticipating changes in the political, economic, and social environment which could require changes in the way business is carried on.

The types of influence that religious organizations can exert may be divided into three categories: sociological, contextual, and organizational (e.g., political influence or power). Sociological influence is that which develops when the faithful attempt to follow clear and detailed rules laid down by the hierarchy of the religious body. Because the rules require a definite response on the part of the follower, sociological impact, as defined here, should be the most easy to trace and analyze. Such rules would include Roman Catholic bans on birth control and abortions; Hindu taboos on killing cows; and Islamic rules requiring prayer sessions five times each day, a month of fasting, or prohibiting women (whether Muslims or not) from operating automobiles.

It cannot, of course, be assumed that such rules are followed equally by all followers of a faith worldwide. Papal statements on birth control are certainly accepted less in the United States than in Latin America. A ban on women driving cars may be overridden by a Middle Eastern or Asian government seeking rapid modernization. But certainly Hindu prohibitions have affected the food supply in the Indian subcontinent and the Catholic ban on birth control is a serious impediment to controlling populations in Latin American countries, an area of rapid population growth and serious nutrition and health services deficiencies. And what long-term consequences must be faced in a country such as Iran, which under the Shah blithely ignored too many fundamental religious taboos in its quest to join the industrial powers of the Western world?

The second type of influence, contextual, is that which flows from the personal beliefs and convictions of the individual faithful as to how life is to be lived or how events should be interpreted. The best examples of research in this area are the efforts by Weber[3] and Tawney[4] to develop the theory of a Protestant work ethic.

While extremely difficult to study empirically, the contextual impact of religion has been acknowledged and respected literally for centuries. With the exception of their problems in Palestine, the Romans were intitially very successful in ruling a vast empire in part because they were careful to respect a diversity of religious beliefs.[5] For his expedition to Egypt in 1798, Napoleon had both the Bible and the Koran included in his traveling library under the heading "politics" and was careful to instruct his staff officers in local religious practices.[6]

Vern Terpstra in his book *The Cultural Environment of International Business* argues that religion "is the most important *single* variable in explaining economic development."[7] The Farmer-Richman model of international management stresses the important effects cultural factors, one of which is religion, can have on the practice of management abroad. Other articles have demonstrated that important relationships exist between work and nonwork facets of life, showing that social structures within a society can have clear impacts on individual personal reactions to work and other domains of life.[8] Most, if not all, religious groups emphasize thrift, hard work, and the absence of indulgence as qualities to be sought by the faithful. Such qualities, encouraged by religious institutions outside of the work place, are, of course, also valuable qualities for productive workers.

Examples of contextual influence can be found easily even in the U.S. A federal district court judge in Minnesota has called for repentance by corporations. The influence that religion has had on his beliefs and outlook, the contextual influence, was clearly evident in his references to several of the Ten Commandments in berating the business community.[9] Voting behavior in the United States Congress also shows indications of being tied to religious beliefs.[10] One study shows how Japanese and Korean firms have developed structures that are compatible with, or replace, traditional familial hierarchical structures paramount in the Confucian system.[11] Such a development should certainly be of interest to researchers and practitioners who would suggest that Japanese or other management structures could be beneficially transferred, in whole or in part, to other cultural environments. As Kenneth Boulding pointed out, "the success of economic institutions depends to a large extent on the nature of the whole culture in which they are embedded, and not on the nature of these institutions in themselves."[12]

Examples of efforts by religious organizations to exert political influence, the third type of influence which they enjoy and a primary focus of this study, abound in recent news events. Berger and Neuhaus clearly point out the importance of religious organizations as well as the problem, mentioned earlier, of overlooking their importance, stating that: "Religious institutions form by far the largest network of voluntary associations in American society. Yet, for reasons both ideological and historical, their role is frequently belittled or totally overlooked in discussions of social policy." These authors also note that "The wall of separation between church and state ... is a myth long overdue for thorough rethinking."[13]

The most obvious example of the political-organizational influence of religious groups probably has to be the events of 1978-1979 in Iran. It has been suggested that the Islamic organization in that country provided the organizational base for the revolution which was pressed by other, non-

Islamic groups. There have been debates about whether Khomeini used the leftists or the leftists originally tried to use Khomeini to achieve their goals. More recently, fears have existed in the Middle East that an Iranian victory in the Iran-Iraq war could destabilize moderate Arab regimes in the area, some of which have Shiite majority populations.[14] In the Middle East in general, Islam enjoys added influence of a political nature from the fact that the Islamic pulpit (called the minbar) has been used for centuries for public communication.[15]

In Poland the Roman Catholic church has enjoyed a unique influence for a nonstate organization in the Communist world. The power of the Catholic church as a counterweight to the government is clearly respected by Polish authorities. This power may have actually increased as the government attempted to clamp down on the activities of independent activists and unions in the country. Outside relief organizations have often required that any aid sent be funneled through the church. Polish authorities have been known to rely on clerics to preach against violence.[16]

In Nicaragua, Catholic Base communities (CEBs) gradually began to move from a focus on the sacraments to a focus on social issues, slowly drawing the formal church into the revolutionary movement.[17] In Brazil, the Catholic church has been an important force to be reckoned with by the government in its efforts to deal with problems such as inflation.[18] The failure of Italy's Banco Ambrosiano brought to light connections with the Vatican that may lead all the way to Latin America.[19]

Of course, we don't need to look overseas to find examples of political-organizational activity on the part of religious groups. Many churches have attempted to influence the activities of U.S. corporations in South Africa. A recent example: in late 1981 the Lutheran School of Theology at Chicago voted to withdraw its accounts from Continental Illinois Bank to protest the bank's involvement in South Africa.[20] The declarations of America's Catholic bishops on nuclear armaments and, more recently, on the appropriateness of various economic policies have been well publicized.

In the U.S. presidential election of 1984, statements by religious leaders sparked controversy as the religious sincerity of both candidates became an important issue. Over the past decade, fundamentalism in the U.S. can hardly be overlooked in discussions of efforts by religious groups to exercise political power. While its actual size and influence is impossible to measure, the "moral majority's" obviously political activities include publication of congressional voting records, financial support of candidates for political offices, boycotting sponsors of certain television programs, and lobbying legislative bodies with respect to issues such as abortion, birth control, and national defense.

While a great deal of evidence suggests that religious organizations are influential actors in the business environment, the problem, as stated earlier, is that a lack of awareness of their roles still exists. This naiveté on the part of many businesspersons, not to mention sociologists and political figures,[21] and a lack of understanding of religious organizations are the broad problems this research seeks to address. The two major purposes of this study are 1) to create an awareness of the relationships of religious organizations to the business and political environment; and 2) to attempt to use existing methods from management and organization studies to analyze a particular religious organization (the Roman Catholic church) in an effort to develop a means for empirically approaching the study of the organizational influence of religious groups. As the Catholic church has frequently been cited as an enduring example of a successful management bureaucracy, a better understanding of this bureaucracy, from an organizational rather than a theological perspective, should provide a valuable addition to the field of management study.

The Plan of the Study

To fulfill its two major objectives, this research will be divided into three main parts. First, the study includes a historical analysis of the development of Roman Catholic economic doctrine and of efforts to apply it to world and national problems. This should not only illustrate the role that religious groups play in the business environment but will also show, in a descriptive and nonempirical manner, the interdependence of religious and political organizations.

The second part of this book consists of an empirical case study of this interdependence. It concentrates on efforts by the Roman Catholic church, on a local (individual diocese) level, to co-opt (or form alliances with) other groups in its environment. More specifically, it attempts to apply the resource dependence model to the in-depth study of a Roman Catholic diocese, the Archdiocese of Indianapolis. If successful, this would represent a previously untried extension of this model and a relatively unique approach to the study of religious organizations.

Finally, a broad-based study of several dioceses in the U.S., through a questionnaire sent to each, was used in an effort to suggest to what extent the conclusions of the case study might be more generally applicable to dioceses across the United States.

The Resource Dependence Model

While specifics of the resource dependence model, the model around which this research is centered, will become clear as the research propositions are discussed, some discussion of this model and its place in this research is necessary at this time.

In essence, the resource dependence model posits that organizations will attempt to form linkages with other organizations on whom they are dependent for critical resources (resources that are necessary for the continued health of the organization, usually necessary to continue production processes). These linkages are made in an effort to improve stability in the supply of needed inputs (or stability in markets and competition) through the influences they provide within other organizations.

Types of linkages that have been studied include such things as placing executives of other organizations on the board of directors of the focal organization (the organization under study),[22] combining with another organization to form a joint venture, activity in professional organizations (such as the National Association of Manufacturers) in which contact is maintained with other firms on an informal basis, and many others.[23] These approaches to linking with other organizations will vary with regard to the resultant amount of influence over the other firm (merger or acquisition, for example, providing a great deal of control and, therefore, a substantial reduction of uncertainty) and with regard to the cost of the method used. Association with a supplier or competitor through membership in a professional organization, for example, will require a very small commitment of resources and time. This will not, however, provide for the same stability of supply or markets as will acquisition of that supplier or competitor. A logical extension of this concept suggests that a greater commitment of time and resources will be made to influencing those organizations most critical to the focal organization. This commitment can then be studied in an effort to assess how a particular organization seeks to exert influence over other organizations in its environment.[24]

This research focuses on the efforts of one unit of one religious organization (a diocese of the Roman Catholic church) to exert influence through such linkages. After a look at the transfer of economic ideas between the Catholic church and society in chapter 2, and the basic organization of that church in chapter 3, chapters 4 through 6 concentrate primarily on the reasons why people are chosen to serve on various diocesan administrative boards. It is expected that, if the model holds true for religious organizations, many persons will be found serving on these boards who can provide ties with other important organizations, rather than providing administrative experience or expertise in a particular field. While the study focuses primarily on one method of linkage, the use of board memberships, other methods looked at provide insights into how a church may seek sway within a community as well as into the way the Catholic organization works.

2

Roman Catholic and Secular Economic Thought: A Brief History

It was not the economists who liberated the slaves or who passed the Factory Acts, but the rash and ignorant Christians.
—Kenneth E. Boulding

The most important challenge for today's church in Brazil is ...political...to build a just society.
—Neil Ulman

Having discussed the importance of religion and of major religious groups worldwide, we will now turn our focus to a deeper study of the Roman Catholic church. Because the rest of this book focuses on the Roman Catholic church we will, for brevity, frequently use the term "the church" to refer to this organization or its units. Chapter 2 discusses, as briefly as possible, the major trends in Western economic thinking, focusing particularly on the church's role in that development. This historical overview is important for three reasons.

First and foremost, by looking at the development of Western economic theory and its relationship to Catholic writing, we add to our appreciation, developed in chapter 1, of the important role a religious group can play in shaping political and economic structures. This chapter provides a longitudinal study that illustrates, in a way that is impossible in the cross-sectional tests described in chapters 4 and 5, the clear impact of the Catholic church on Western thought.

Second (and conversely), this chapter highlights the influence that institutions and events in the church's environment have had on its organization and doctrine. We will see that much of the church's economic philosophy can be traced to the Greeks, whereas its hierarchical structure is closely related to Rome's. Indeed, this history of the church will be seen to support literature cited in chapter 4 that suggests religious organizations act in a manner similar to secular organizations.

Finally, this chapter provides an important foundation for later chapters where we study the church at a lower level of aggregation.

The task before us, to discuss the major trends in economic thinking from Old Testament times to the present, is nothing less than gargantuan and would quickly become impossible unless carefully defined and limited. To develop an understanding of the evolution and present focus of Roman Catholic economic thought, we will trace its development through history and compare and contrast it with two major schools of secular economic thought: laissez-faire capitalism and Marxism. It should be noted that these two systems may not exist anywhere in the world today in the sense in which they will be discussed but are, in fact, theories. These theories attempt to express an ideal which is always modified when put into practice in a real-world setting. The reader must be careful to understand that the comparisons and descriptions that follow do not attempt to deal with the complexities of a political-economic system as it may actually develop, e.g., the industrial capitalism of the United States or Soviet communism.

The comparisons made below are limited to two major dimensions which appear repeatedly in Catholic writing: the *theory of value* (specifically the proper determination of prices and wages, and thus incomes) and the controversy over a *just distribution of wealth* (or the right to private ownership versus common ownership of assets). Other subjects are discussed briefly for the sake of continuity, but our attention remains focused on concerns about value and ownership.

Value and Ownership

The doctrinal position of the Roman Catholic church on value and ownership has remained constant since the time of St. Thomas Aquinas (although, as we will see below, application to the secular world has fluctuated considerably). The primary basis of all value is labor and the major determinant of a just price for a product is that it must yield a fair wage to the laborers involved in producing it. Pope Leo XIII cites theory of value as a basic truth in his famous encyclical *Rerum Novarum*[1] and Pope John Paul II has clearly reaffirmed it:

> Just remuneration for work of an adult who is responsible for a family means remuneration which will suffice for establishing and properly maintaining a family and for providing security for its future.[2]

> To be so poorly paid that you can hardly support yourself and your families, that you become slaves rather than free and responsible workers, this, too, is not just. This is not the will of God.[3]

On ownership of private property, the church has also been consistent in its official position. The church supports the institution of private ownership but cautions that private property is ultimately a trust given to the owner by God. As such, property must be administered for the benefit of all people and not for the purpose of selfish gain.[4] Church scholars have often emphasized this point when berating the system of capitalism.

Capitalist economic thought originally agreed with the Catholic concept that labor is the basis of all value.[5] Later modifications have, however, argued that value is determined in the marketplace by the interaction of supply and demand. Marshall argued that while this relationship is complex and subject to many influences, prices will, in a free market, move toward a point at which they are stable, the point at which supply and demand are in equilibrium.[6] The price of inputs is then derived from this price, labor being considered a major input.

Marx, on the other hand, argues that labor continues to be the ultimate basis of value.[7] While better developed and more complex than Catholic labor value notions, Marxism is very similar to Catholic thinking on this dimension. Marx, like Catholic social thinkers, complains of inequities that are created by a capitalist philosophy which turns laborers into commodities that are exposed to "all the vicissitudes of competition, to all the fluctuations of the market."[8]

Marx would, however, strongly disagree with Catholicism on the subject of private property. He sees the accumulation of private property in the capitalist system as "the expropriation of the peasantry" and as "the act of violence that inaugurates the capitalist mode of production."[9] He claims that the institution of communal property is an ancient one[10] and paints attractive pictures of associations "of free men, working with the means of production held in common."[11]

All three systems (capitalism, Marxism, and Catholic doctrine) are efforts to develop a set of guidelines which will improve human life. Catholics differentiate themselves from both of the other systems claiming that Catholic social doctrine views individuals as *human* beings while capitalism and Marxism see instead *economic* beings.[12] The church argues that improvement of human life can come only through attention to human dignity.

... the fundamental criterion for comparing social, economic and political systems is not, *and cannot be,* the criterion of hegemony and imperialism: it can be, and indeed must be, the *humanistic criterion,* namely the measure in which each system is really capable of reducing, restraining and eliminating as far as possible the various forms of exploitation of man and of ensuring for him, through work, not only the just distribution of the indispensable material goods, but also a participation, in keeping with his dignity, in the whole process of production and in the social life that grows up around that process.[13]

By contrast, capitalist theory argues that improvement in the human condition will come through increased productivity, which is the result of the power of economic self-interest. Marxism claims that redistribution of wealth and common effort will produce the desired improvement.

Table 2-1 summarizes the major stands of the three groups. Our discussion has been brief and has made broad distinctions, glossing over many of the complexities of these three very different strains of thought. As we move through this chapter, these gaps will be filled and at least some of the complexities of each school will be considered. At this point, however, it is important to establish the major positions and to understand that areas of both agreement and disagreement exist between Catholic and capitalist schools and Catholic and Marxist schools. In other words, the official position of Roman Catholic economic and social doctrine is neither capitalist nor Marxist. By the same reasoning it is not totally incompatible with either system.

Table 2-1.   Major Economic Positions of Capitalism, Marxism, and Catholicism

System	Basis of Value	Basis of Ownership	Critical to Human Improvement
Capitalism	Market Equilibrium	Private	Improved Productivity (Growth in the Surplus)
Marxism	Labor	Common	Redistribution of Property and Incomes
Catholicism	Labor Cost	Private but Should Benefit All	Attention to Human Dignity

Ancient Philosophies

Both secular and Roman Catholic economic doctrines can trace their roots to the ancient world. It is, therefore, logical to start there in looking at the development of each.

Biblical Contributions

The foundations of economic thought are not really economic at all. They are, in fact, attempts to describe the social order and the consequences of life on earth.[14] The economic process in the times of the Old Testament was so simple as to require no explanation. Economic theory, as we have come to know it, containing the concepts of capital, labor, supply, demand, rent, interest, profit, and so forth, didn't begin to develop until the end of the seventeenth century—relatively recently in human history.[15] During much of the period between Old Testament times and the development of the above modern concepts the church provided the major, if not the only, source of economic philosophy.

Old Testament laws and Hebrew thought mirror a conflict between a communal tribal society and a more complex society which was divided into classes and castes based in large part on the ownership of private property rather than something to be held in common.[16] As the economic climate changed, the Prophets began to revolt against the disintegration of the primitive community and communal property, which came to be replaced by private property and a marked distinction between rich and poor. During this period the Hebrew monarchy developed, supported by the tolls and profits from the king's growing foreign trade.[17] The Prophets saw these developments as a movement away from God and "by their denunciation of the covetousness of the new society they sought to guide men back to the way of living of the covenant, to revive justice and mercy as the principles of social behavior."[18] They didn't realize that the existing order had become inappropriate and so could only call for a return to simpler times. While the biblical Prophets could clearly see changes that were occurring in the social order, they did not understand the forces underlying these changes.[19] This rather reactionary response to social and economic change, and a desire for stability and preservation of the existing system, can be seen not only in the writings of early biblical teachers, but in those of other ancient philosophers and Christian writers as well. During the Old Testament period many of the ideas which were to clearly emerge at a later time, and particularly the debates over property and distribution of wealth, saw their earliest expression. Even though the discussions were not basically economic in nature, many of today's Christian writers look at Old Testament philosophies and the Gospels for guidance when discussing human interest questions.

The Greeks

Toward the end of this same period, Greek philosophers, notably Plato and Aristotle, were also writing what were essentially analyses of the social order. These, too, would have a great deal of impact on later economic thought. Like those of the Prophets, Plato's writings were basically concerned with utopian social order reform, not with economics. Plato strongly supported a caste system in which a ruler class trained to be philosopher-kings should dominate a class made up basically of artisans. This recognized changes which had led to the development of the city-state, specialization, and trade. Plato argued that the city arises because of the division of labor, which was itself the result of natural inequalities in human skill and the multiplicity of human wants.[20] Plato's account of the division of labor is his main contribution to economic theory.[21]

Eric Roll calls Aristotle, Plato's pupil, "the first analytical economist."[22] Aristotle's contributions include an attempt to define the scope of economics, an analysis of exchange, and a theory of money. According to Aristotle, economy is divided into two parts: economy proper (the science of household management) and the science of supply (the art of acquisition).[23]

Aristotle's discussion of household management focuses on the development of the city from the household and village. As in Plato's writings, the state is divided into rulers and ruled, the rulers being the statesmen, magistrates, and priests, while the ruled are the farmers and laborers. The basis of the city was slavery, which Aristotle justified by claiming that some people were slaves by nature[24] (they were to be recruited from people of non-Hellenic origin).[25]

In his discussion of the second part of economics, the science of supply, Aristotle analyzes the art of exchange. His theory of exchange value only grudgingly allows for trade as a necessity in the ideal city, for he regarded it as an unnatural occupation.[26] He is primarily concerned with the point at which further exchange, or trade, becomes unjustifiable. Aristotle emphasized that "people should cease trading when they have enough" and he concentrated on the question "of the principles determining the number of units of commodity X that are, in some sense, 'equivalent' to one unit of Y, Z, etc."[27] The achievement of justice in exchange, the *fair* value of one commodity exchanged for another, would become the concept of "just price" in the Middle Ages[28] and Aristotle one of the sources of Canon Law.[29]

Aristotle defined economic surplus as a vague concept having to do with a volume of real output over and above some psychological or physiological estimate of minimum need.[30] This emphasis on trading limited to the fulfillment of needs, the advice that people should cease trading when they have enough—that to gain more than is needed is unnatural, can be seen as a reflection of economic and social conditions during the period in which Aristotle wrote (ca. 384–322 B.C.). During this period (the decline of Greece set in after 400 B.C.)[31] there was a lack of ability or incentive in the city-states of Greece to expand the economic surplus. If the surplus is static or declining, then one's loss is another's gain. The pursuit of profits in this situation is proscribed because one person can only gain when another loses. Such a loss may prevent the latter individual from fulfilling a position in society, ultimately leading to the collapse of society as a whole. This assumption, that the economic surplus could not grow (based on his experience within the environment of decline at the time), led to Aristotle's concern with distribution as expressed in his concepts of fair exchange as noted above.[32] As we shall see, many of Aristotle's views on fair exchange, his concerns about equitable distribution, would be adopted by "Scholastics" writing during a period of similar economic stagnation in the Europe of the the late Middle Ages.[33]

Both Plato and Aristotle, to somewhat differing degrees, defended class, private property, and, to a lesser extent, trade. They injected, however, an ethical aspect which argued that the owners of property had certain moral responsibilities: there were right and wrong uses of wealth or property and right and wrong uses of money. Money's purpose was exchange—not the earning of more money through interest. Aristotle sees money as a store of value which is "serviceable with a view to future exchanges."[34] Once again it is both interesting and informative to pause here and note that all of these ideas will eventually find their way into early Catholic doctrine, illustrating the importance of environmental as opposed to canonical impacts in shaping Catholic economic thought.

Rome and the Life of Christ

Rome left a meager legacy of economic discussion but did establish some important precedents for classical thought. Not until the decline of Rome was there again a concern with economic questions. The influence of the environment on thought may again be seen, this time in a perceptible change in the view of slavery. Coincident with the end of the periods of conquest and decline in the supply of fresh slaves, the whole economic basis of slavery was destroyed and slavery came to be questioned as an economic institution.[35]

Perhaps the most important development during the Roman period was the significant increase in commerce and, subsequently, the development of laws for its protection. Roman law stressed unrestricted individualism and upheld the rights of private property almost without limit (in stark contrast to the views of both Plato and Aristotle). Because of this emphasis Roman law serves as an important basis for the legal doctrines and institutions of capitalism.[36]

During this same period the life of Christ (which has recently come to be a central focus of some Third World movements, such as Liberation Theology) took place and was recorded in the Gospels. Christ's mission as emancipator of the poor and oppressed is today the subject of much debate. The Gospels do, however, proclaim the worthiness, both in a material and spiritual sense, of *all* work and seem to withdraw support of caste systems or any sort of inequality.[37] While one might logically expect that these teachings would provide a major source of Christian economic doctrine, it is interesting to note that:

When we reach the Middle Ages we find that the words of Christ are no longer enough as a basis for the doctrines of the Church, which, embodied in the Canon Law, held sway over the whole of men's conduct. In addition to the ethical percepts in which Christ's social teaching had originally been contained, the doctrines of Aristotle, derived from a different historical background and inspired by different motives, form the foundations of medieval thought.[38]

In other words, Roman Catholic economic doctrine as it would develop in the Middle Ages was not handed down from God. It was, rather, the interpretation by the early Christian writers, whom we shall refer to as the canonists, of the philosophies of many different worlds as modified by the situation and institutions of the declining Roman Empire and the Middle Ages.

The Canonists

Virtually all of the major issues which set apart Catholic, Marxist, and capitalist economic thought were introduced by the time of Christ. All three positions on the basis of ownership had been defined before Christ: communal ownership had been defended by Old Testament prophets; private property administered responsibly for human good had been advocated by Plato and Aristotle; and pure private property had been supported by the Roman system. The seeds of both labor and utility theories and market exchange theory of value had appeared in the works of Aristotle.

The period of the canonists coincides with the decline of the Roman Empire and the development of the nation-state in Europe. It was during this period that the church enjoyed its greatest power in secular affairs. The church grew and eventually filled the vacuum left by the retreating Western Empire.[39] It provided some sense of stability and uniformity in a Europe of small principalities which were not entirely unlike the Greek polis.[40] Once again the total volume of production was relatively constant; the economic surplus was static or declining. Any acquisitive instinct had to be curbed as one person's gain would be another's loss. The "temporal and secular power of the church was, therefore, invoked to prescribe 'justice' in commercial transactions."[41]

With its initial development under the canopy of the Roman Empire the church also became power-minded and linked to the state. It has been argued that the force which came to be used by the Crusaders and the Inquisitors was not accepted by the church as legitimate until after Constantine, the emperor who first accepted Christianity.[42] This led to a major change in the church's actions and position in society.

Confronted by the powerful, (the church) seeks alliance and resorts to compromises ... it came (after Constantine) to be one institution among others in the Western world ...[43]

In studying the development of Catholic economic doctrine it is important to be aware of the many sources of influence outside the church which helped shape its teachings. From the preceding statements, as well as from interviews conducted in this research, it is clear that the hierarchy of the Roman Catholic church was modeled on that of the empire, the church's hierarchy developing primarily after it became a "legitimate" institution with Constantine, its concept of justice growing from the Greek and Roman concepts.[44] Historian Barbara W. Tuchman notes the influence which secular actors began to have on the church of Rome when she states that "by Constantine's gift, (of endowments in lands and leases, lordships and servants) Christianity was both officially established and fatally compromised."[45]

She moves on to indicate that this relationship with the secular world continued after the fall of Rome itself:

> ... conflict between the reach for the divine and the lure of earthly things was to be the central problem of the Middle Ages. The claim of the Church to spiritual leadership could never be made wholly credible to all its communicants when it was founded in material wealth. The more riches the Church amassed, the more visible and disturbing became the flaw; nor could it ever be resolved but continued to renew doubt and dissent in every country.[46]

Tuchman also gives evidence of how this relationship influenced church teaching during the period.

> The (manorial) system was aided by the Church, whose natural interests allied it more to the great than to the meek. The Church taught that failure to do the seigneur's work and obey his laws would be punished by eternity in Hell, and that non-payment of tithes (during this period usually a portion of what you produced, e.g., grain, eggs, a hen or pig, given in support of the church) would imperil the soul.[47]

This early evidence of a dependent relationship between religious and secular authorities (the church receiving land and other favors in return for aid in maintaining some control over the peasants) should help to dispel any notion that religious organizations are able to remain separate from secular affairs, i.e., the notion of church-state separation. Catholic writers often reacted to events and influences of their times just as did other economic thinkers such as Adam Smith or Karl Marx.

The early Christian writers restricted their writings on economic reform to the advocacy of restraint in the pursuit of riches, just behavior in business, and generous but voluntary almsgiving to the poor.[48] Society in the Middle Ages, like the society of Greece, was highly stratified, each person in theory having his or her proper place.

To the medieval theorist... one did not work to "make money" in the modern sense—for money could be made in this sense only by cheating someone else, by taking more than one's rightful share.[49]

Christian writers, in a manner similar to the Old Testament prophets and the Greek philosophers, wrote in support of maintaining the social status quo and the divisions which existed to their benefit. Theodoretus, writing in A.D. 435, argued in essence that different persons had different functions and that inequality in the distribution of wealth was a mode of social organization which yielded both to the poor and the rich a more agreeable life.[50] Other Christian writers indicated that the existence of rich and poor segments of society was in accordance with the wishes of God. The existence of each class provided the other with the opportunity to exercise the virtues appropriate to that class. In the case of the rich, the proper virtue was charity toward the poor. The poor were to exercise patience and humility with respect to the rich.[51] Almsgiving, therefore, while a specifically religious obligation, was meant only to relieve extreme distress and not to eliminate poverty, seen as necessary to society.[52]

Slavery is seen by the Christian writers as a legitimate and useful institution, a view held without major modification until the end of the eighteenth century. Slavery is viewed as a punishment and, to some extent, a remedy for sin. Contrary, however, to Aristotle, slaves are not by nature seen as inferior species of human beings. They are believed to have the spiritual quality of human beings; the dignity of human personality could not, therefore, be justifiably withheld from them.[53] Labor has value in that it promotes moral discipline but is not valued for its contribution to productivity.[54]

No father seems to have recognized the possibility that income or property in excess of current need might help the poor more if used productively... than if distributed as alms.[55]

Paralleling Plato and Aristotle, the canonists are hostile to trade or commerce (a position which they inherited from Greek and Roman writers). They see no economic or moral justification for the derivation of income from purely middleman activities. Some do, however, see value in trade insofar as it provides social contacts between peoples, leading to better unification of Christians in Europe. Theodoretus recognized that the lower costs and reduced difficulty of transport by sea might be real benefits of overseas commerce.[56]

During this period the views of Plato and Aristotle on the rights of private property were adopted by Christian writers. Being the chief landholder in Europe,[57] the church was certainly not interested in any sort of a redistribution. In fact, during this period the church confronted a number of heretical sects which were giving a decidedly communist interpretation to the Gospels.[58] In attempting to put down these movements, St. Augustine and others argued that giving up possessions was not required for entrance into heaven, as these sects demanded.[59]

The Christian writers do, however, attach responsibility for society's welfare to the ownership of property, the position still held by the church today.[60] This position may be summed up in the words of St. Jerome, who states that "your possessions are no longer your own but a stewardship is entrusted to you... "[61] The Council of Gangra, held in the fourth century, concluded that:

> ... renunciation of the goods of the earth was not required of the simple faithful Christians; they need only give alms. *The Church did not despise riches if managed by their owners with justice and benevolence* [emphasis added].[62]

This position was later incorporated into the Theodosian Code, which made Christianity the official state religion of the Roman Empire.[63]

Augustine carried the doctrine of stewardship further by arguing that dominion over all things belongs to the righteous. This doctrine would be used later in denying the property rights of heretics and infidels and was eventually turned against the church itself. Although the church ultimately rejected St. Augustine's position when it adopted the doctrine of natural rights of individuals to property,[64] its general stance on the proper basis of ownership had been expounded by the Christian writers by the end of the fourth century A.D. and would be repeated by St. Thomas Aquinas in the early 1200s.

St. Thomas Aquinas

St. Thomas is clearly the dominant influence in all of Catholic economic writing. As recently as 1917 the Code of Canon Law (which was replaced in 1982 with a new promulgation) stated that "professors of philosophy and theology in seminaries, etc., shall teach 'according to the argument, doctrine, and principles of St. Thomas which they are inviolately to hold.' "[65] St. Thomas believed that "Aristotle's philosophy contained the essential truth about the natural world" and, therefore, "made his bold attempt to reconcile it with Christianity."[66]

There were a large number of similarities between the Greece of Aristotle and the Europe of Aquinas. Both societies were composed of relatively small and fragmented political units (the Greek city-states as opposed to the fiefs of the feudal lords); both societies were experiencing low or declining economic growth; trade was limited if it existed at all; and both societies were on the verge of a drastic change in their political structure (in the case of Greece the conquest by Macedonia, leading to its merging into the "larger" Hellenistic world; in Europe the development of the nation-state and mercantilism). A major concern for both Aristotle and Aquinas was the preservation of stability in a disintegrating environment.[67] In his pursuit of stability Aquinas adopted many of the positions of Aristotle, whose works were just appearing in Latin translations in Western Europe.[68] Aquinas condemns usury, as did Aristotle. He supports slavery, as did other Christian writers, with the relatively slight modification of the Greek position noted above. Aquinas also adopted the position found in both Plato and Aristotle that communities, or states, arise from the fact that people have different abilities and are social animals that can fulfill themselves only within the context of some social or political unit.[69]

Of most interest to us, however, is Aquinas' theory of just price. As with Aristotle, Aquinas' major concern is for justice in individual transactions and for maintenance of the status quo.[70] The proper price for an item is based on 1) the value of the labor which was put into it, and 2) the materials used in the production.

It should be noted that in Aquinas there is more specification of production costs than in Aristotle. His is, therefore, not a pure labor theory of value (those who view it as labor value have called Aquinas the philosophical forerunner of Marx).[71] Others have suggested that Aquinas was aware of the market price (a capitalist concept) and considered it "just" but assumed that this market set price would revolve around his own just price. While not a pure labor theory of value, Aquinas' analysis did, however, place a great deal of emphasis on the contribution of labor and this emphasis can be seen in Catholic writing.[72]

In Aquinas' theory of just price, as in Aristotle's, the labor units are weighted by their relative worth. The relative worth of different types of labor is determined, at least in part, by the laborer's position in society. As a result, in Aquinas' theory, the labor of a knight is certainly valued more highly than that of a cobbler.[73] Related to this, St. Thomas' theory of a just wage states essentially that laborers should be paid an amount which will enable them to maintain their stations in society.[74]

Both Aquinas' theory of just price, with its concern for the relative values of different types of labor, and his theory of just wage fit well into the purpose of maintaining the social status quo. The proper price of an item is based on the value of labor and supplies used, while the value of labor is linked to society's estimate of the social value of the labor. Like earlier medieval writers and Aristotle, Aquinas also condemned the acquisitive instinct and disdained commercial activity. Also like Aristotle, he placed emphasis on the minimization of wants.[75]

As we approach the end of what is called the Middle Ages, and the decline of the canonists, we can see that the current positions of the church on economic matters have been clearly developed, primarily by Aquinas. On the subject of the basis of ownership of property he and earlier church writers repeat Aristotle, stating that private property is a legitimate institution but should be treated as a trust given by God for the benefit of all. Aquinas' theory of just price is a kind of labor cost theory of value.[76] Both of these positions are shown in table 2-1 (p. 12) as the major positions of the Catholic church today.

In addition to these positions, the Christian writers and individual scholastic theologians condemned the acquisitive instinct[77] and trade. Aquinas condemned usury, a position the church held (but did not always adhere to) until the middle of the nineteenth century.[78]

Most important, perhaps, was the development of an underlying concern with a proper distribution of wealth rather than with the possibilities of increasing the wealth of all through an increase in productivity.[79] Early Christian writers such as Aquinas are not concerned with the inequities between rich and poor, and they fail to see the possibility that higher productivity can improve everyone's existence. Today, a very potent force in much recent Catholic social thought is a concern for just distribution, as opposed to the Aristotelian proper distribution which emphasized a distribution in line with position in society rather than based on the worth of the individual as a human being. Now, as then, Catholic theory fails to consider the possibility of improvement through productivity growth.[80,81]

Development of a Secular Economics

The period between the fall of the Western and Eastern Roman empires, approximately A.D. 500 to A.D. 1500, was the period in which basic Catholic doctrines with regard to the economic world were formed. A central element of Catholic moral theology—the maxim that the common or public good had priority over individual good—was codified at this time from roots in the writings of Cicero, Seneca, and Aristotle.[82] St. Thomas' writings have been referred to by popes in social encyclicals and in the codex of canon law.[83] This same period, however, was one of decline for the church in terms of its influence. With the Renaissance came changes in society which were in conflict with Catholic ideology. The harmony of church dogma and society came to an end with the end of feudal society.[84] Aquinas marked both the climax of the development of Catholic metaphysics and the beginning of its fall. Nonreligious philosophy received its sanction with the organization of the four faculties at the University of Paris, an event that occurred during St. Thomas' lifetime.[85] The advent of the nation-state with its new systems of governance and increasing desire to engage in commerce was fought by a church that had become one of the greatest of feudal landlords.[86,87] The Catholic church, bound by its long tradition and supranational character, was not amenable to these changes or to temporal economic doctrines and, therefore, fell relatively silent.[88,89] At the end of the Middle Ages "though attempts were again to be made to introduce ethical elements into the main stream of economic thought, it (remained) henceforth independent of religion."[90] The foundation for a secular science of economy had been laid.[91]

In justice to some of the later canonist writers, it should be noted that they did begin to allow that a competitive market price best reflected the fair price of a commodity. The *communis aestimato* basically suggested that if a merchant sold goods for the current price in a market the price was fair. This was because where many buyers and sellers met there arose a common price based on many judgments which, it was felt, was the just price for a given market.[92] Schumpeter observed that this price theory was later "explicitized" into the price mechanism of classical economics.[93] Nevertheless, this development has never been recognized by the church as a part of its doctrine.

While some writers were beginning to implicitly recognize and allude to the possibility that market forces may lead to a just price, a theory that value should be determined by market forces would not be produced for some time. Throughout the mercantile and classical periods price would continue to be connected to labor value or to some combination of costs including labor.

Mercantilism

Mercantilism, the first identifiable secular school of economic thought, represented a strong change from the writings of the early church and the Greeks. With the development of the nation-state and the great maritime discoveries of the Portuguese, Spanish, English, Dutch, and French came a great expansion in commerce. While writers such as Aristotle and Aquinas had frowned on trade as, at best, a necessary evil, it was now believed to be the only possible way to create an economic surplus.[94] This period saw the development of the great trading companies—Muscovy, the Merchant Adventurers, the East India Company, and others. The state itself was largely a creature of commercial interests whose aim was to have a strong state provided they could manipulate it to their exclusive advantage. For this reason most pieces of mercantilist policy were put forward identifying the merchants' profit with the national good.[95]

Many of the mercantilist writers were merchants themselves and defenses of the practices of their companies can be seen in their writings.[96] Monopoly, for example, supported in many writings, was accepted as legitimate and would not be questioned until the end of the eighteenth century, and then only in England.[97] It is interesting to note that in this period (as with the canonists of the Middle Ages, Aristotle in Greece, and the writers of the Old Testament times) the writers seem to be primarily concerned with supporting and preserving a present status quo that is favorable to them. They tended to overemphasize short-run interests.[98]

Possession of an abundance of gold and silver was an important goal of policy. There developed an almost fanatically exclusive concern with selling, the "fear of goods" characterizing mercantilist thought. In England mercantilists whose desire was to preserve the stock of precious metals and who favored the control of specie flows and the revival of the office of Royal Exchanger were referred to as bullionists. A member of this school, Edward Missleden, first coined the term balance of trade.[99] It was, however, left to classical economists to connect prices, specie stocks, exchange rates, and the balance of trade into a comprehensive theory of international trade.[100]

The mercantilist period does not contribute anything directly to the position of the three schools of thought on the variables with which we are concerned. It neither improves on theories of value nor directs itself to a consideration of the effects of distribution. The importance of mercantilist theory and policy was that it abolished medieval restrictions, particularly with respect to commerce and the charging of interest, and helped to produce unified and strong nation-states.[101]

The stage for the development of classical economics was set by the development of philosophical thought and scientific inquiry. Among the philosophers, Thomas Hobbes argued that the individual, impelled by self-interest, was the motivating force for societal improvement.[102] John Locke went on to argue that the natural form of organization for purposes of government was the orderly, voluntary association of merchants in commercial ventures.[103] He also claims that the basis of freedom "was property, acquired by industry and reason, and entitled to the security which the state could give."[104] This, according to Eric Roll, is "the philosophy of triumphant capitalism."[105]

The scientific method of inquiry was also developed during this period. This was the period called the Enlightenment, which saw great advances in science by persons such as Isaac Newton, Benjamin Franklin, Voltaire, Leeuwenhoek, and others. The physiocrats in France were the first to apply consistently the scientific methods of isolation and abstraction to economic inquiry. Later, Smith and Ricardo could use them consciously as analytical tools.[106]

Once again, however, developments on the theories of value and distribution would wait for a later period. Locke argues that legitimate property should be limited by the amount that individuals need for their own maintenance,[107] essentially a position already taken by both Aristotle and Aquinas. Sir William Petty claimed that all real wealth arose from land and labor, whereas the physiocrats in France believed that land was the only source of net economic surplus.[108] As regards this position of the physiocrats, it is enlightening to note that physiocracy was a "fad" in France in the late 1700s which represented a reaction to heavy, repressive taxation and to inequalities in the distribution of wealth. The physiocrats argued, therefore, that land should be taxed directly. Such a program would have shifted financial burdens to the nobility.[109]

The Classical Period: Smith, Ricardo and Malthus

The classical period of economic inquiry was introduced in 1776 by Adam Smith with his treatise *An Inquiry into the Nature and Causes of the Wealth of Nations.* Smith and David Ricardo are the dominant figures in the classical school, although many other famous authors, including Karl Marx, are considered classical economists. Smith's philosophy was accepted widely and rapidly primarily because it explained basic truths of the period. It was also in agreement with the growing industrial classes which desired greater freedom in their dealings than was acceptable under mercantilism, which tied commercial interest closely to the interests of the nation-state.[110]

During the classical period economic thought became less ethical and more analytical. Land and labor (in both Smith and Ricardo) and labor (in Marx) were identified as the ultimate sources of productive power. In some respects this seems, again, to be a reversion to Aristotle and Aquinas. However, minimization of wants and a desire to maintain the status quo are no longer the ends desired.[111]

The system of private ownership probably receives its most eloquent support in Smith. He puts self-interest at the center of human conduct as the motive which inspires everyday business life. Smith argues in favor of the abolishment of state regulation and intervention and against monopoly, all of which is in the interest of the most progressive classes of the time.[112] "Economic progress was dependent upon the establishment of the independence of the industrial capitalist."[113] Such theories were to reign supreme in the Western world for more than a century and a half, and many today still refer to Smith when seeking to defend the institutions of private property and private enterprise.

As we have suggested, theories of value did not progress much beyond those of Aristotle and Aquinas during this period. Smith originally designates labor as the sole source of value,[114] but his logic is confused and several different stands may be identified. In his discussions, after first identifying labor as determining the relationship in exchange between different objects, Smith also allows for the value of materials and the profits of stock.[115] He thus develops a price called the "natural price" which is based on the cost of rent for land, wages for labor, and profit for stock.[116] He claims later that this natural price or value is the central price to which the prices of all commodities are continually gravitating, recognizing that supply and demand in the marketplace combine to affect what the actual price will be.[117] Nevertheless, while allowing that market forces do impact *price*, Smith still seems to conclude that the proper *value* of commodities is ultimately tied to the costs of land, labor, and capital,[118] a position not unlike that of some of the later church writers.

Ricardo's theory of value is also somewhat confused. He argues that the original source of exchangeable value is based on the quantity and difficulty of the labor required to obtain it. He also points out, however, that the price of labor, the amount of other commodities which it will command, can vary with the scarcity of labor.[119] This says, in essence, that the value of a commodity depends on the amount of an input, labor, which itself can vary in value. He also argues that the labor value, which determines the amount of other commodities which a commodity will command, includes not only the immediate labor but also the labor that goes into supplying the implements for the production and transporting of the materials needed.[120] He indicates that the value of capital arises from the quantity and quality of labor which produced that capital, and that the profits which go to capital are simply the just compensation for wages foregone during the nonproductive period when the capital stock (e.g., machinery) was being produced.[121]

Another theme that arises in the writing of Ricardo is a concern with distribution of wealth. "Ricardo is mainly concerned with the distribution of wealth under conditions of increasing scarcity."[122] He believed that economic growth would continue for some time (unlike Aristotle and Aquinas, who were living in already stagnant societies) but at a decreasing rate until some stationary point was reached. There were two reasons behind this belief: 1) the niggardliness of nature—output in agriculture would rise but at a decreasing rate as less productive land was brought into tillage—and 2) the passion between the sexes which would increase the population.[123] Concerned with this predicted stagnation Ricardo believes, like Aristotle and Aquinas, that when one person is able to acquire more goods it will necessarily reduce the riches of others unless the productivity of labor can be increased.[124]

Ricardo's theories were influenced by Thomas Malthus, who clearly spelled out similar concerns in *An Essay on the Principle of Population*. Malthus concluded that when the population became too large there would be an oversupply of labor. This would lead to a reduction in wages. With wages dropping, family size would decrease as a result of the inability of workers to support large families. Malthus believed that people would marry later, thereby shortening the period during which children were conceived; he further postured that at the same time a shortening of life spans would occur as a result of living conditions in growing urban areas.[125]

Smith, Ricardo, and Malthus, while concerned with contemporary problems, believed strongly in existing institutions and felt that the cause of poverty lay in bad laws which encouraged inefficiency and fecundity. However, John Stuart Mill and Karl Marx, also members of the classical school, are "far less (willing) to accept the immutability of existing social forms."[126]

The Classical Period: Mill and Marx

Mill was very critical of wealth and landed interests and he defends early versions of communism (the monastic orders, the Moravians, the followers of Rapp), claiming that people knew only of their problems but not of their resources.[127] He also complains that while we speak of the "laboring class" out of custom, a laboring class can only exist where there is also a "nonlaboring class" (appearing to confuse landlords and capitalists with nonlaboring groups). He argues that the relationship between nonlaboring and laboring classes is traditionally of a benevolent nature (e.g., parent-child), which must end with education. Mill also suggests the elimination of pure capitalists and the institution of cooperative ventures where profits are divided according to the individual's contribution to the effort.[128] He does not, however, argue in favor of the elimination of competition as did socialists of that time.

Marx attributed all evil to existing social forms and argued that their abolition was not only necessary but also inevitable.[129] He felt that the capitalists, the owners of the capital which was necessary for production, were exploiting the laboring class. "Capitalist production brings about the expropriation of individual producers whose private property was based on their own labor."[130,131] Marx's theory of "primitive accumulation" claims that capitalists did not become capitalists because of superior intellect and energy but, rather, through this exploitation of the individual producers.[132] His theory of immiseration decrees that the poor will become absolutely more poor leading to a growing differential between rich and poor.[133]

Within the classical period, then, we have the exposition of most of the values listed in table 2-1. The Roman Catholic positions on both value and property were, of course, set earlier. Both the capitalist and Marxist positions on property were also developed primarily during this period. Smith, Ricardo, and Malthus argued in favor of the institution of private property while Mill and, of course, Marx decried the accumulation of large amounts of property in the hands of the capitalist. Mill, as was noted earlier, argued in favor of some system in which the laborers themselves could share ownership.

In the case of the theory of value, all positions except the modern capitalist position were developed by the time of Marx. Mill started out with Smith's value in use and value in exchange (utility of an item and its power of purchasing other goods respectively) and goes on to argue that the value in use must always exceed the value in exchange or a person would never purchase a commodity.[134] He also defines price as value in money, differentiating it from value or exchange value which is set in terms of other real goods which can be obtained by its exchange.[135] While, like Smith, coming close to the concept of market value, Mill goes on to argue that value is related to the cost of production (labor, materials, etc.) plus some reasonable profit. This, he claims, determines minimum exchange value, a point on which actual exchange value will center in a competitive environment.[136] Picking up on Ricardo,[137] Marx claims that both the source and measure of value is labor.[138] So while exchange in competitive markets is recognized as influencing price, at the end of the classical period the belief that value was ultimately determined by the quality and difficulty of labor input, or by some combination of labor and other factors, was still predominant.

From 1848 to 1871 there were few significant developments. Malthusian population theory became more and more suspect during the 1850s and '60s, at least in England, where living standards were rising in the face of increasing population.[139]

The labor-based theories of value also became weaker during this period. Economics became far more cosmopolitan during the later part of the nineteenth century, and outside of England classical economics was coming under increasing attack. The classical school tried to explain the value of commodities in terms of other "commodities," the costs of which were themselves subject to variation. Classical theories could not handle the logical possibility that the factors of production (land, labor, capital, and entrepreneurship) should be subject to the same general laws that govern the values of the end products.

The "New" Economics

The contribution of W. Stanley Jevons and the Austrians was the discovery of a single basic explanation of value applicable to all commodities and factors of production.[140]

> ... value is not determined by past efforts ... costs accommodate themselves to wants, not the other way around ... factors of production receive their value (i.e., their cost) from the value of the final commodity they help to produce ...[141]

In other words, it is not the cost of the factors of production which added together determine the value of the final product, but rather the price which the final product can command in the market which will determine how much is paid to the various factors. Jevons argued that pleasure and pain were the ultimate objects of the calculus of economics which needed to be expressed in terms of utility. He introduced the idea that an object has utility but also that the utility at the margin decreased with each additional unit until added quantities of a product could produce no pleasure and, therefore, could not command a price in the market.[142]

In his theory of exchange Jevons argued that value expressed nothing but a ratio, and that, therefore, the value of gold (or labor, land, capital, and entrepreneurship for that matter) was meaningless unless expressed as a ratio to something else.[143] He specifically debunked labor theories of value, arguing that labor affects value only insofar as it affects supply, supply affecting the degree of utility which in turn governs value—the ratio of exchange.[144]

It was left to Alfred Marshall, the "great reconciler," to bring together the theories of Jevons and several others to describe a system of value set by exchange in markets. Extending the idea of marginal utility, he states that there is one general law of demand:

> The greater the amount to be sold, the smaller must be the price at which it is offered in order that it may find purchasers; or, in other words, the amount demanded increases with a fall in price, and diminishes with a rise in price.[145]

Marshall also spends a great deal of time describing the relationship between supply and demand. While it is impossible to do justice to his treatment in a very short space, he does provide a summary of the theory of equilibrium of demand and supply. He points out, essentially, that different producers have different advantages in producing an item. The price, therefore, must be sufficient to cover the expenses of production of the least efficient producer. If they do not, then that producer will leave the trade which will reduce supply. Reduced supply should increase the marginal utility of the products produced resulting in a higher price in the market.[146]

Finally, Marshall closes with a discussion of the shortcomings of capitalism noting that we should not give in to utopian ideas which make unrealistic assumptions about human nature. He also cautions against the temptation to overstate economic evils of "our own age."[147]

With Marshall we have come to the point at which all of the variables in table 2-1 have been developed and explained. While other economists after Marshall, notably Veblen and Keynes, have added a great deal to economic theory, detailed discussions of their inputs are not necesssary for our purposes. One important point needs to be made, however, before moving on. Underlying all of Marshall's analyses was an assumption of stability. This assumption is also present in Smith and in groups today who decry government interference in business. Both Veblen and Keynes raised serious questions as to the validity of this assumption, on which pure laissez-faire capitalist theories are based. Veblen, for example, argues that the motive of invidious comparison leads individuals to constantly desire greater accumulation of wealth so as to compare favorably with others. If Veblen is correct then no general increase of wealth can ever satisfy demand or adequately reduce poverty. Veblen also introduced the concept of conspicuous consumption under which people make expenditures for the purpose of enhancing their standing relative to others.

Keynes suggests the possibility that imbalance can occur in areas such as saving and investment, the movement of wages in response to other economic variables, and price changes which can lead to such problems as involuntary unemployment during periods of equilibrium.[148]

The reason Keynes and Veblen are mentioned is to point out that, like Marxist and Catholic doctrines, which have already been subjected to certain criticisms, the capitalist position is itself not without fault. Had nothing been said beyond Marshall, there was a danger of creating such an erroneous impression.

Catholic Social Thought: The Church Breaks Silence

While it is probably inaccurate to suggest that the church was silent during the development of secular economic theories, it is certainly true that it was forced to take a back seat. Its economic doctrine remained substantially unchanged as it fought internal corruption and the force of the Reformation. Nation-states clearly dominated events on a continent which had, 400 years earlier, shown deference to Rome.

The Social Encyclicals

The church propelled itself back into economic matters when in 1891, almost the same year as Marshall published his *Principles of Economics*, Pope Leo XIII wrote *Rerum Novarum* (On the Condition of the Working Man). This encyclical represents the first official writing in a flow which has come to be referred to as "Catholic social doctrine."[149] In part a reaction to fears of added encroachment on church rights by national governments, this doctrine forges close ties with Aquinas[150] and the Gospels while also providing some degree of legitimation for modern Liberation Theology movements.[151]

In the latter half of the nineteenth century, Catholic writers across Europe began to show renewed concern with proper wage levels. Cardinal Manning and Bishop Bagshaive of England, Baron von Vogelsang, Prince von Lichenstein, and Count Lowenstein of Austria, and Leberatore of Italy were all Catholic writers who struggled with the question of what would be a fair minimum wage.[152] Baron Wilhelm Emmanuel von Ketteler, Bishop of Mainz in Germany, considered workers to be victims of the industrial revolution. He vehemently criticized the "evil effects of economic liberalism." "Labor," he said, "has become a commodity subject to the laws of supply and demand."[153] Of course, many modern economists would probably agree with the bishop and note that this has been the case for quite some time. Nevertheless, the Catholic church has consistently condemned a system in which wages were set in an impersonal market. John Callahan, a priest writing in the middle part of the twentieth century, concluded, in essence, that:

1) Given the familial fertility of labor, an employer, if able, has a strict obligation in natural or commutative justice to pay a familial wage, *economic wage theories to the contrary notwithstanding* [emphasis added].

2) Given the inability to pay, workmen and employers have a serious duty to initiate or to cooperate in the exercise of whatever virtue or virtues are necessary to remove the obstacles preventing labor from producing due fruit, familial wages.

3) Given the absence of cooperation on the part of employers, *workers may be under grave obligation to enter a union to further their cause* [emphasis added].

4) Finally, agents of the state have a strict obligation to see to it that the natural strict right of laborers is assured, both by remedial and preventative legislation.[154]

Leo XIII shows the impact of the earlier Austrian, English, and Italian writers in pronouncing the thought of Aquinas to be the foundation of official Catholic philosophy.[155]

However, Leo's writings, and for that matter all of the social encyclicals, deal with a much broader system of concerns than just proper wage levels. *Rerum Novarum* condemns the "callousness of employers" and the "greed of unrestrained competition."[156] It also condemns socialism and contains an elaborate defense of private property.[157] The impact of labor and workers' rights movements can be easily seen in Leo's concern with labor hours and protection of the poor.[158] Leo's position is interesting in that while both his predecessor and successor, Pius IX and Pius X respectively, were intransigent against the socialists, Leo's position contained elements favorable to both socialists and capitalists. This ambiguity makes Leo's position amenable to numerous interpretations, providing the church with flexibility in the chaotic environment of Italy during this period.

While such concerns appear to reflect the impact of labor unions and a general reaction to the conditions of the industrial revolution, *Rerum Novarum* has also been accused of reflecting other, less laudable concerns. Stephen J. Tonsor has accused Catholics of this period of trying to revive the past, which had escaped them with the decline of feudal times. He argues that "much of the opposition to capitalism and industrialism was based on the fact that capitalist human relationships were so ignoble when compared to feudal paternalism and industrialism, so ugly when compared to the fantasy, freedom and elegance of pre-industrial society."[159] He says that "Christian Socialism in England is an effort to re-establish the community and the esthetic sense which characterized pre-industrial England."[160] Tonsor also claims that "it was the German revival of medieval social forms which directly influenced the development of 'social-catholicism' and supplied the basic institutional formulations of *Rerum Novarum* and *Quadragesimo Anno* (Reconstructing the Social Order, Pius XI)."[161] Tonsor suggests that "one has the unmistakable impression that the authors (of the encyclicals) were writing for Italian peasants rather than the industrial workers of Manchester, Essen, or Pittsburgh."[162] There is good reason to believe that his last statement is creditable. Peter Nichols points out that Italian affairs have exercised a weighty influence in the formulation of papal policy.[163] This would be important at the time of the writing of *Rerum Novarum* because the Italian peninsula (and to a lesser extent Germany) was slow to develop both economically and politically. While the rapidly changing conditions in England may have had a progressive influence on men like Smith, Ricardo, and even Marx, the relatively stagnant conditions of Italy would, logically, have had a conservative influence on church writers of the time.

If Tonsor's analysis is accurate, it allows us to make an interesting link with earlier Catholic thought in terms of motives. Once again we find that the principal writers are concerned with promoting a system which provided for a stable and safe environment for the church. This, of course, would be the position that any organization, religious or secular, would be expected to take, to attempt to promote any environment which is supportive of its existence and prosperity. Early Christian writers and medieval theologians like Aquinas, and now more modern Catholic writers including Leo and other popes, appear to consistently espouse the same philosophy. While, if adopted by others, this philosophy might possibly benefit the human condition, it also is advantageous to the church itself. Peter Nichols suggests that this is a very conscious effort, arguing that "this has been the traditional role of the Church: deal with anyone as long as the Church's position is enhanced as a result."[164]

The church's position on private property has often been cited as additional proof that the church would, like any organization, give priority to its own welfare and only secondarily to genuinely spiritual concerns. As noted above, Leo provided an elaborate defense of the institution of private property in *Rerum Novarum*. Pope Pius XI in *Quadragesimo Anno* also defends private property, suggesting that it was given to the individual by the Creator. In a position reminiscent of the earlier canonists, Pius goes on to argue that there are two purposes for the Creator's gift. One is that private property is beneficial to the individual, but the second is that, through the individual, property might be beneficial to society as a whole.[165] He points out that "a man's superfluous income is not left entirely to his own discretion"[166] but also says that "the division of goods which is effected by private ownership is ordained by nature itself."[167]

Like *Rerum Novarum, Quadragesimo Anno*, which was published to mark the anniversary of the earlier encyclical, also takes up concern with proper wage levels. Pius states that the wage paid the laborer must be sufficient to support both the laborer and the laborer's family. He does add a realistic note of caution by stating that the condition of any particular business and its owner must also be considered. "The exigencies of the common good finally must be regulated with a view to the economic welfare of the whole people."[168]

Pius XII, after World War II, voices a principal concern of Catholic social teaching. He felt that many social problems could be solved through the just distribution of property. While this may sound like a drastic change in the Church's position on private ownership, it is really no more than the continued effort by the church to steer a "middle way," showing concern for abuses of the industrial system while still defending private ownership. Pius XII did not advocate government redistribution of property, but rather a more natural redistribution which he felt would result from attention to a just wage. He argued that the principal factor contributing to a better distribution of property would always be a just wage, since this would automatically bring about a more reasonable redistribution of wealth.[169] As Leo did earlier, Pius charted a position which was amenable to numerous interpretations. He justifies the institution of private property, an obvious interest of the church, while not entirely excluding socialist concerns from his writing. This is interesting in a pope traditionally viewed as intransigent against socialism and communism.

John XXIII in the encyclical *Mater et Magistra* (Christianity and Social Progress) again takes up both the issue of a just wage and that of private property. Like Pius XI, John says that both the needs of the worker and his family and the condition of the business must be taken into account when determining what makes up a just wage.[170] Pope John does clearly recognize that several factors, and not just labor, contribute to the nature of any product. He sees that a portion of the value of any product should rightly belong to those responsible for directing private enterprise. But he also argues in favor of decreasing the disparity between rich and poor.[171]

John's position on private property appears to be very close to that of his predecessor, Pius XII. He does, however, place much greater emphasis on achieving a just distribution than does Pius. John argues in favor of efforts to improve the distribution of ownership, but cautions that prudent efforts must be made toward this end using "various devices already proven effective." While giving the state the role of supervising these efforts for the common good, Pope John also cautions that safeguards must be set up "lest the possession of private citizens be diminished beyond measure, or, what is worse, destroyed."[172] Again we see a pope taking a position which is ambiguous and, therefore, can be interpreted favorably by many constituencies.

Pope Paul VI in *Populorum Progressio* (On the Development of Peoples) and *Octagesima Adveniens* showed concern for "the lack of brotherhood among individuals and peoples." Paul VI seemed to feel that this, rather than monopolization of resources by a small number of persons, was the real root of the problems of the twentieth-century world.[173] In *Octagesima Adveniens*, rather than attempting to provide answers to these problems (e.g., by staking out a position on proper wages, property rights, etc.), Paul VI attempts to raise "the consciousness of individual Christians to their duty to respond to the problems of the poor and the oppressed, to protect the values of liberty, personal responsibility, and openness to the spiritual or transcendent."[174]

John Paul II places emphasis on human dignity. He is a strong advocate of proper respect for and treatment of laborers. He has given several speeches on this subject and his third encyclical, *Laborem Exercens* (Performing Work), is devoted to concerns of dignity and proper treatment of workers. The current pontiff states the "principle of the priority of labor over capital," reminiscent of the classical school of economics. He argues that in the process of production "labor is always a primary *efficient cause*, while capital, the whole collection of means of production, remains a mere *instrument* or instrumental cause." He concludes by stating that "this principle is an evident truth that emerges from the whole of man's historical experience."[175] Contrary to Jevons and Marshall, John Paul II cautions that we must not treat labor simply as a special kind of merchandise, but rather that we treat man as the purpose of the whole process of production (i.e., "as a person [man] works, he performs various actions belonging to the work process" as part of God's call to subdue the earth and dominate it while moving toward self-realization)[176] rather than as an instrument of production.[177] As did Aquinas, Popes Leo XIII and Pius XI, and John Callahan, John Paul II calls for a just wage to be determined by need of the worker.[178]

John Paul II has been considerably less vocal on the issue of private property. In *Laborem Exercens* the pope attempts to differentiate the church from the capitalist position by noting that the church has never held that the right of property is absolute and untouchable. He also, however, condemns collectivism. The position of John Paul II seems to be a logical extension of that of his predecessors. Like Aristotle and Aquinas, John Paul supports the concept of private ownership but points out that "the right to private property is subordinated to the right to common use."[179] But, like Pius XII and John XXIII, John Paul II has also expressed concern with the unequal distribution of wealth:

The drama (of world hunger) is made still worse by the presence close at hand of the privileged social classes and of the rich countries which accumulate goods to an excessive degree... [180]

As can be seen, the basic positions of Aquinas are still intact though modern interpretations have provided somewhat new shadings. Even though some of the late canonists did seem to recognize that some, perhaps most, markets set prices, strong emphasis has been placed on the role of labor. Similarly, the most recent Catholic teachings, while not specifically espousing a labor theory of value, do place human beings at the center of the work process and make labor a primary cause of production.

Catholic writers have also been careful to steer a course between absolute rights for holders of private property on the one hand, and the elimination of ownership on the other. While often condemning what was felt to be an unjust distribution of wealth, official Catholic doctrine supports slow adjustment based on a fairer wage system, allowing more people to enjoy ownership of land and the means of production, rather than any sort of drastic redistribution by force. This would obviously protect the rights of property owners, among which the Catholic church must be included, while providing recognition of liberal complaints against "Western exploitation" as well. Throughout this period of Catholic social writing we see an active effort by the church to stake out a position with respect to contemporary economic issues, but that position has always contained elements which make it amenable to numerous interpretations and, therefore, does not entirely alienate any particular group.

Before leaving a discussion of Catholic social thought, two other developments need to be discussed: the development of Catholic attitudes toward socialism, Marxism, and capitalism, and the importance of the Second Vatican Council.

The Church and Modern Political Economy

The Roman Catholic church originally reacted strongly against both socialist and Marxist movements. Arthur McGovern has suggested that this reaction can be explained by the church's fear of liberal social revolutions. This fear built up over a period of hundreds of years.

The Reformation had challenged Church authority, the Enlightenment introduced pernicious secularized values, the French Revolution subordinated the Church to the state, and laissez-faire capitalism had destroyed the harmony of guild structures. Socialism seemed bent on carrying these disruptive ideas and tendencies to their radical conclusion, the destruction of all that is sacred, holy, and "natural." [181]

Leo XIII and Pius XI both condemned liberal capitalism but Pius also condemned socialism as replacing free competition with economic dictatorship.[182] Then, shortly after Stalin had purged, imprisoned, or executed millions of people, Pius XI released *Divina Redemptoris* (19 March 1937). This encyclical "promulgated a condemnation of 'Atheistic Communism.'"[183]

The postwar years marked the strongest period of anticommunism in church history. A decree by the Holy Office under Pius XII in July 1949 forbade Catholics to either join or to encourage the Communist party in any way. It also forbade the faithful to publish, distribute, or even read books and papers which upheld communist doctrines.[184]

With Pope John XXIII, however, Catholic anticommunism was to soften. In his encyclicals, Pope John spent very little time condemning false ideologies and instead attempted to promote practical responses to the world's problems.[185] Both John XXIII and Paul VI were interested in pursuing a sincere dialogue with governments and leaders which their predecessors had, only recently, vehemently condemned. Agostino Cardinal Casaroli, currently the cardinal secretary of state who, as John XXIII's secretary of the Council of Public Affairs, masterminded this policy, notes that communism is clearly atheistic and a threat to religious liberty worldwide. Nevertheless, he claims that, in pursuing a dialogue "the Church is following its traditional policy of not giving way on essential principles but remaining ready to look at possibilities of practical agreements."[186] In other words, the church is careful not to alienate important constituencies.

This mellowing of church policy took place against the background of growing unrest in less developed countries and an increase in the use of Marxist analysis in the rhetoric against "Western imperialism." Pope John Paul II, who is clearly not supportive of communist movements, seems to be guilty of believing the "Marxist fallacy." In *Laborem Exercens* he states that:

> Throughout this period of [Catholic social] teaching which is by no means yet over, the issue of work has of course been posed on the basis of the great *conflict* that in the age of, and together with, industrial development emerged between *"capital" and "labor"*...[187]

The belief that this great conflict really exists is virtually the Marxist position and is discounted by many Western economists. Nevertheless, in a church and pope which have traditionally been quite cool to Marxist ideologies, we can clearly see the influence of Marxist analysis. McGovern notes that "Christian commitment would seem to demand being partisan to the poor and the oppressed; but such commitment also risks the loss of objectivity."[188] Nichols notes that the church has, in a sense, been forced away from strong anti-Marxist attitudes. He notes that the church needs to be wary of taking positions which, in the Third World, might force it to repeat the "eighteenth century mistake of opposing social unrest and eventually revolution by supporting the absolute monarchies...as the bulwarks of Christian civilization."[189] By taking a strongly anti-Marxist or anti-communist position instead of trying to analyze and work with followers of these ideologies, the church would risk making exactly such an error. If a revolution were to be successful, the church would probably need to face repercussions against both church property and the faithful in areas such as Latin America and Africa.

Impact of Vatican II

This brings us to the subject of the Second Vatican Council, a meeting of the world's Catholic bishops called together by Pope John XXIII in the early 1960s. One cannot do full justice to an event as large as this in church history in only a few words. Vatican II sought to place the church "in" the world.[190] As Nichols notes, the Roman Catholic faith is a very "westernized" religion.[191] This remains true today even though less than half of the Catholic faithful are in First World countries. In the very near future, Latin America alone will have half of the world's Catholics. By the year 2000, Third World countries will contain 70 percent of the world's Catholics and 90 percent of the world's population.[192] The pope himself is not from the "modern West" as we normally think of it. When Polish Cardinal Karol Wojtyla was elected pope in 1978, non-Europeans outnumbered Europeans in the College of Cardinals for the first time in its history.[193]

As these trends continue, however, Rome is seen by some non-Western Catholics as another symbol of Western imperialism. A priest from Bangkok, Thailand, said that he could not stand to look at "those monuments to imperialism."[194] An African priest complains that "his people, by being converted from Europe, were risking not ever becoming properly Christian *in African terms* at all" [emphasis added].[195]

Vatican II addressed these and other issues. The church as an institution theoretically became much more open and flexible. It taught that the pope was not alone in governing the church but that he was, essentially, only the first bishop among equals.[196] The decree on missions encouraged greater dialogue with the people the church serves and a greater awareness of cultural differences. The council directed that

> In order to be able to consult more suitably the welfare of the faithful according to the condition of each one, a bishop should strive to become duly acquainted with their needs in the social circumstances in which they live. Hence, he ought to employ suitable methods, especially social research.[197]

In discussing diocesan boundaries, council documents show concern for cultural or other natural groupings and provision, it is noted, should be made for the faithful of different language groups.[198] Vatican II also suggested the establishment of a pastoral council in each diocese to include lay people as well as clergy. It encourages bishops to consult priests "for the sake of greater service to souls."[199]

All of these changes, if effective, should lead to a greater responsiveness on the part of the official church to "grass roots" concerns of the faithful. Following this to its logical conclusion, we would expect the Catholic church to be influenced to a much greater extent by Third World economic and political philosophies and conditions as the population shifts mentioned earlier continue to occur. This would, indeed, be a significant change in what has, up to this point, been a large and conservative Western institution. Nichols, however, suggests that, for all of the effort and good intentions of Vatican II, the changes have been chiefly cosmetic.[200] He shows how the bureaucracy of the Roman Curia has worked against a larger role for bishops in governing the church, one of the goals of Vatican II.[201] He suggests that the failure of Vatican II

> ... looks like another piece of evidence for the innate conservatism of deep-rooted institutions. When institutions are weak, they cannot change themselves. Reform is too much. When they are strong, they no longer want to... [202]

If we look back at the major tenets of Catholic economic doctrine, which have been stable since before Aquinas, we would agree with Nichols' conclusion. But a closer look at the different "shadings of meaning" these tenets took on with the passage of time (as described above), at the church's changing position with regard to the legitimacy of different political and economic philosophies, or at the influences which seem to be at the root of these positions would cause us to form a different opinion. While the church is unquestionably a very conservative institution, there is evidence that, like any other organization, it does respond to environmental pressures that threaten its survival. Thus, while Vatican II may not have had the impact some had hoped, the pressures on the church to move in the direction that was mapped out are probably as great as any the church has faced. Consequently, as population pressures increase it is logical to expect some change. Given the openness to the faithful encouraged by Vatican II and the location of much of the faithful in the Third World, it is logical to project that much of the church's hierarchy will move toward a greater empathy with the problems and positions of Third World peoples. Such movement can be seen in positions espoused by Pope John Paul II on his trip to Latin America in early 1985. This could have important implications for Western business people and multinational corporations because, at the very time that the Catholic church seems to be becoming more politically active, it is likely to be influenced in its teachings more and more by people from areas which often subscribe to Marxist analysis.

Conclusions and Trends for the Future

At the beginning of this chapter we attempted to spell out briefly the positions of three major "schools" of economic thought with respect to their theories of value and their positions on the institution of private property. On value, capitalist economics argues that proper value is exchange value set in a free market, and that the value of all inputs including labor is derived from this figure. Marx, on the other hand, claims that both the source and the measure of value is the amount of labor invested in a product.[203] The Catholic church, while not holding exactly to the Marxist position, espouses a theory that is fairly close to it. In a sort of labor cost theory the church recognizes that inputs other than labor must be considered in determining a product's value. Nevertheless, John Paul II in his encyclical letter *Laborem Exercens* insists that labor is the primary efficient cause of production.[204] Thus, while technically different from the Marxist position on value, Catholic doctrine does parallel it fairly closely.

The capitalist position on private property is that it is an absolute right which must be protected. The Marxist position is that the capitalists have acquired their vast holdings of wealth and property by robbing the proletariat of the proper fruits of their labor. The Marxist remedy for this abuse is collective ownership by the proletariat. The Catholic position on this issue is more evenly balanced between capitalism and Marxism than is the church's position on value. The church supports the institution of private property as long as holders of property understand it to be a gift from God which is to be employed for the benefit of all. Recently, however, the church has grown more and more concerned with a "more equitable" distribution of ownership, a position which, again, seems to lean closer to Marxist rather than capitalist analysis.

Having looked at the development of these three trends of thought, it should be obvious that many of the greatest authors were influenced by events in the contemporary environment and by a desire to protect their own position. Several of the mercantilists held positions with major trading companies and their writings reflect support for a system which was profitable for those trading monopolies. Old Testament writers, Plato and Aristotle, St. Thomas Aquinas, and it appears the German Catholics and Pope Leo XIII, all wrote in support of either the status quo or of an older system of political economy that provided more personal and institutional stability. In this one respect the Catholic church can be seen reacting to environmental change in a way that is quite similar to the reaction of most large organizations.

It is also evident that the church's position has not, in fact, remained unchanged since Aquinas. Aquinas clearly did espouse a labor cost theory and gave labor a dominant position in his theory of just price. He does not, however, claim that labor is the primary cause of production. And while the basic position on private property still stands, Aquinas was never concerned with the inequitable distribution of wealth, a distribution which was, if anything, more inequitable in this time.[205] Aquinas and other canonists did, in fact, adopt the Aristotelean position that each class, including slaves, had an important role to play if society was to run smoothly.[206] It is, however, enlightening to note that these new shadings of the Thomistic positions on value and property have developed coincident with the church's efforts to open itself to the Third World and with an increase in the use of Marxist analysis in the Third World.[207] Most recently, as was mentioned above, Pope John Paul II espoused the Marxist fallacy that there exists a worldwide struggle between labor and capital.

While the relationships mentioned above do not prove that the church has, in fact, adopted changing approaches to economic analysis in response to outside pressures, they do certainly raise some interesting questions. If a critical resource for the Catholic church is its membership, its membership base is rapidly shifting to the Third World and particularly to Latin America. At the same time, while much of its financial support comes from the West, its membership in those countries, if not falling, appears to be becoming less loyal. If we assume that the Catholic church seeks survival and some measure of prosperity (not to mention protection of its people and property rights in the emerging Third World), then this shift in its economic doctrines is clearly logical considering current demographic trends. Pfeffer and Salancik note that

> The ability of the organization to link its interests or activities to the current social norms may be the most important aspect of ensuring its interests are served.[208]

There is also evidence that the church is active, beyond its declaration of official doctrine, in attempting to influence events in its favor.

In many areas of the world, national or even regional episcopal conferences have grown in importance since the Second Vatican Council. Examples which come to mind are the National Conference of Catholic Bishops in the United States and CELAM in Latin America. In Canada, however, during this same period the national episcopal conference has become weaker while provincial conferences have become stronger. This may be due in part to the French Canadian separatist movement. Nichols suggests that the Catholic church has been critical to whatever success the French separatist movement has had.

> If the Catholic Church had failed to defend the position of the French in Canada, the British would not have been forced to respect this huge enclave of old-fashioned European culture in the midst of the New World.[209]

Nichols also notes that the Canadian church took up the Indian cause with respect to the route of the Trans Alaskan oil pipeline and got the route changed.[210] Monsignor Alexander Carter, a bishop of Sault Sainte Marie, Canada, has been outspoken in his criticism of multinational corporations. Although he was cut off while speaking against them at the Synod of Rome in 1971,[211] his position is certainly compatible with officially expressed concerns about unequal distribution of wealth. Pope Paul VI came out strongly against aspects of capitalism because he felt it must bear a great deal of the blame for increasing injustice in both rich and poor countries in the world. Additionally, John Paul II has consistently attacked the permissiveness of consumer society.[212]

In the United States, predicts Nichols, the Catholic church will eventually take up the position of other Catholic regions in condemning multinationals.[213] He also suggests that, while it is weakening today, collaboration between the Catholic church and the trade unions has traditionally been strong. "Andrew Greeley sees the unions as the other crucible, with the parishes, in which American Catholicism was formed."[214] This author's personal interviews with Catholic prelates seem to confirm such a trend. While Catholic immigrants at one time accounted for a major share of U.S. labor, their descendants have, in many cases, moved into middle class white collar jobs. As labor becomes "less Catholic" it would also be logical to expect a smaller amount of interaction with the Catholic church.

The church has on occasion extended its influence by joining with other religious groups on various issues. One example is the Nestlé boycott, which received significant support from several church groups, unions, and health organizations. This effort has been a factor in changes made recently by the company.[215]

In Poland the Catholic church has been the forerunner in the reestablishment of the "flying university," which has grown into a "veritable semi-institutionalized youth movement whose discussions are as broad as the issues confronting Polish society."[216]

Other examples of Catholic political activity on a personal or an organizational scale abound. Brazil's Catholic church has been active in supporting a Worker's Party candidate who calls capitalism a system of death which, he says, must be destroyed.[217] Catholic priests and nuns have been killed, kidnapped, or harassed in some way in several Third World countries as they fought with others for social change. Pope Paul VI, in *Populorum Progressio*, accepted the right of revolutionary uprising in case of "evident and prolonged tyranny"[218] (although John Paul II has spoken firmly against violent activity).[219]

This chapter has described a church which, while maintaining that the writings of Aquinas are official doctrine, has unquestionably shifted to the left in its interpretation. A recent poll of Catholic seminarians in the United States indicates that 57 percent of them believe that "repressive regimes backed by the United States" are a greater problem than communist expansionism. A majority believe that economic abundance is best achieved by redistribution rather than by growth.[220] (It should be pointed out, however, that these figures, being part of an editorial comment, are difficult to substantiate.)

This chapter has also shown us a church which appears to act like many other large organizations. Its doctrine seems to be motivated, in part, by a desire for stability. Recent doctrinal shifts appear logical in light of the assumption that the church, like any organization, is seeking to realign itself with a changing power base. And recent actions by the church suggest it to be an organization that, if not actually acquiring more power, is seeking to reassert itself in world affairs. Unsubstantiated but interesting reports about the Vatican Bank's involvment with Banco Ambrosiano and John Paul II's dialogue with the Soviet Union over Poland certainly raise the possibility that the church is becoming a more potent force in the world. While the church has often attempted to use political influence, events such as Ambrosiano indicate that it is now also seeking to exert economic power where it may be useful as well. This combination of a changing economic philosophy and a more secularly active church could conceivably have major ramifications for multinational corporations seeking to do business in Third World countries, and particularly in Africa and Latin America.[221] The church in these areas may provide an organization which can consolidate opinion and provide a source of organizational strength for interest groups which previously were only able to enjoy minor, if any, policy influence.

Let us now review briefly the three goals of this chapter so that we may structure and clarify what we have covered.

Initially, we stated the three purposes of this chapter as follows: 1) to look at the role of Catholic teaching in the development of Western economic thought, illustrating the impact a religious group can have on the political and economic environment; 2) to look at the impact that the environment has had, conversely, on the development of Catholic doctrine; and 3) to add to our understanding of this complex and enduring institution. Clearly we now have a somewhat better understanding of the Roman Catholic church, having studied its social and economic teachings. Chapter 3 will add to this understanding by describing the structure of the worldwide Catholic church and its units in preparation for a case study of one of its local units, the Archdiocese of Indianapolis.

Looking at the other two purposes of this chapter we do clearly observe a great deal of two-way organizational-environmental influence. Early Christian writers clearly are an important source of Western economic thought. Positions which they (and their successors such as Leo XIII and John Callahan) have taken are reflected in all schools discussed in this chapter. Modern European labor theories of value in particular originate with church writings.

More importantly, however, we can also see the important impact which the environment has had in shaping Catholic positions. Positions found in Thomistic writings can be traced, almost intact, to Aristotle, a clearly pre-Christian writer. The roots of recent Catholic teaching often seem to be in fear of further loss of power by Rome or in the economic and political events of Italy. Writings of the church are frequently ambiguous and subject to many different possible interpretations. This would seem to reflect a desire for a flexibility which would contribute to survival in a world of conflicting interests. The current cardinal secretary of state, Agostino Cardinal Casaroli, has stated that the church's traditional policy has, in fact, been one of pursuing a dialogue with groups seen as hostile to the church and of seeking possibilities for practical agreement.[222]

A clear awareness of important actors in its environment, the desire to accommodate them when theologically possible and permissible and the clear evidence that the church's policies are shaped, at least to some extent, by its environment: these findings provide the basis for the subsequent chapters. The present chapter illustrates that the Catholic church, contrary to some myths, is very much a part of its environment and that it survives, in part, by remaining open and designing some flexibility into its positions. In this it is clear that the church has much in common with other secular organizations which have been studied by organizational theorists to a much greater extent. We will now move to a study of local units of the Roman Catholic church. Using some of these techniques we will study more closely the units' interactions with their local environments and the impact of these interactions on structure.

3

The Church's Formal Structure

We assume... that religion as a social system possesses the characteristics of an organization...
                                                            —L. Vaskovics

It should now be clear that churches can organize in different ways, and in ways that are relatively distinct from those found by the original Aston studies and by many of the extension studies.
                                    —R. Hinings, S. Ranson, and A. Bryman

The Roman Catholic church is, among other things, a vast, complex, long-standing and bureaucratic organization. It is doubtful that anyone fully understands this complex organization so it is necessary before studying it, or any part of it, to attempt to develop some common base from which to proceed. To do this the present chapter will describe, very briefly, the basic aspects of the formal structure of this institution. Subsequent chapters will then move to study the less formal adaptations made by the church in dealing with its environment.

The Roman Catholic Church as an Organization

This discussion will be divided into two parts: 1) a discussion of the administrative structure of the church internationally (the Roman church), and 2) a discussion of the local divisions of the church (the dioceses and archdioceses). One of these local units, the Archdiocese of Indianapolis, is the primary subject of much of the research to follow.

The Church Internationally

Figure 3-1 provides a simple depiction of the organization structure of the international (or Roman) church.[1] Since Vatican II, the church has emphasized a more collegial structure with the pope occupying the position of a bishop who stands as "first among equals." In figure 3-1 this relationship is shown by the linkage of the box "Individual Bishops with Ordinary Authority" to the rest of the structure by dotted rather than solid lines. This is meant to indicate a communication rather than a command or superior-subordinate relationship. Nevertheless, bishops generally have little power in the central administration of the church[2] and therefore, the low position given to the bishops and their representative organizations in the diagram. A bishop with ordinary authority is a bishop who is placed in control of a diocese. The structure of a typical diocese is discussed later and is shown in figure 3-2.

The administrative structure in Rome was established by Pope Sixtus V in 1588[3] and has undergone relatively moderate change since that time. The main changes have been the development of the secretariat of state and its subsequent move to a central position in the hierarchy. There has also been the addition of many secretariats and offices to the original set of congregations.

Administratively, the three most important men in the structure are the cardinal secretary of state, his assistant—the substitute and secretary of the cypher—and the secretary of the Council for Public Affairs.[4]

The secretariat of state controls and coordinates most of the activities of the other offices and congregations. It has developed into a kind of prime minister's office for the papacy, running the government in Rome while also being involved in most of the contact with units of the church worldwide.

The nine sacred congregations function as a set of staff departments in the church. They provide information to the pope on such issues as selection of bishops, clergy concerns and problems, and evangelism. They may solicit information from bishops and, in their areas of competence, they may enjoy some line authority (e.g., the Sacred Congregation for Catholic Education with respect to seminary operations). The sacred congregations were composed entirely of cardinals until Pope Paul VI introduced bishops into service in the congregations. However, the prefect (or head) of each congregation must still be a cardinal. The cardinals who are heads of the congregations also serve on a coordinating and advisory committee which is presided over by the cardinal secretary of state.

Secretariats have been added to the Vatican structure since the establishment of the sacred congregations and have sometimes been referred to as the "New Curia." They function in a way that is very similar to the sacred congregations. Because they are much newer they do not, however, enjoy the status of the congregations and are not always run by a cardinal.[5] An example

Figure 3-1. Vatican Organization Structure

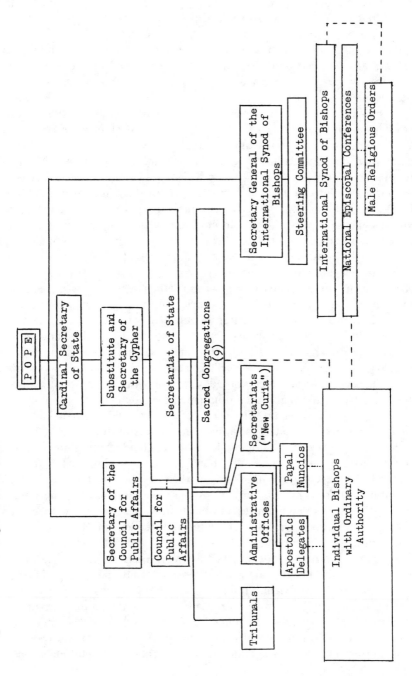

of a secretariat that deals with a current concern of the Catholic church is the Secretariat for Promoting Christian Unity.

The administration in Rome also includes offices (such as the General Statistics Office of the Church or the Prefecture of the Papal Household) which deal with day-to-day operational concerns. The Roman Tribunal acts as a court for the interpretation of canon law and provides for the establishment of regional tribunals.

The secretariat of state sends papal representatives to the nations of the world as a sovereign state sending ambassadors to other countries. These representatives are given the title of papal nuncio if they serve in a country with which the Vatican has official relations (the United States established diplomatic relations with the Vatican in 1984). In countries which have not established diplomatic ties the representative is called an apostolic delegate. The Vatican has also established a permanent observer mission to the United Nations. These representatives, in addition to their diplomatic roles, also serve to communicate papal concerns and requests (but not commands) to individual bishops. While it is easy to assume that a cardinal who is an apostolic delegate has authority over a bishop this is not officially true. A cardinal is the title given to a bishop who may then help to elect a pope but this does not confer additional "line" authority on the holder of this title.

The Roman Curia is the group of cardinals who serve in Rome in the various administrative capacities mentioned above. The college of cardinals includes the curia as well as all other cardinals, the majority of whom serve as ordinary (bishop) of a diocese as well. The college of cardinals elects the pope when the need arises and is composed of men of many different nationalities. The curia has traditionally been dominated by Italians.

Since Sixtus V set up this system of governance cardinals have been predominant in church administration. With the pastoral emphasis of Vatican II, however, there is a developing desire to give the bishops a greater voice. During his administration Paul VI began to add bishops who were not cardinals to the congregations and, in 1965, established the International Synod of Bishops. This is a body of bishops which is chosen by the national episcopal (bishops') conferences and meets in Rome once every three years. Not a governing body, the International Synod is called purely for the purpose of consulting with the pope. It elects a steering committee which acts in the absence of the entire body during the three-year interims between meetings of the whole synod. The secretary general of the International Synod of Bishops is chosen by the pope. Nichols points out that the synod has not been relied on very heavily by the Vatican, the cardinals still being the dominant powers in the church's administration. He notes, however, that the synod is a much more cosmopolitan body than the curia and, if employed more often by popes for consultation could lead to a greater world awareness by the church in Rome.[6]

National episcopal conferences are organizations which include all bishops in a particular country. These have become much more popular and active since Vatican II although some, such as the National Conference of Catholic Bishops in the United States, have existed in some form since the turn of the century or before. Orders of religious men (e.g., Jesuits, Franciscans, etc.) send representatives to both the national conferences and to the International Synod (religious women are not yet included).

Like any bureaucratic organization the Vatican organization may get out of control under weak leadership.[7] The functions of the heads of the congregations and many offices in the network cease, however, on the death of a pope. A new pope could, therefore, appoint an entirely new curia. In addition to this the pope must reconfirm all appointments every five years. At least in theory, therefore, if not always in reality, the pope has considerable power over this administrative apparatus.[8]

There are four major sources of financing for the activities of the Vatican. First, the Vatican holds a number of stocks which were given by Mussolini in compensation for the loss of the Papal States. This is the most important source of income in the Vatican's official budget. The second major source of funds is the Peter's Pence. This is an offering given by the people of the entire Catholic church through the dioceses every July 29—the feast of St. Peter and St. Paul. The size of this contribution varies with the popularity of the papacy, providing some incentive to choose a popular pope. German and U.S. churches are the chief contributors to the papacy via this offering. Income from investments provides a third, although relatively small, source of income. Interest tends to be low due to a conservative investment policy and a desire not to appear crassly commercial. The final source of income is the sale of stamps which provides for the administration of Vatican City.[9]

The church also conducts special drives in the United States to pay off the bills of Vatican II, a campaign which continues today. There is also some flow of funds directly between local, regional, and national segments of the church (e.g., from U.S. churches to African churches) although this is frowned on by the hierarchy.[10]

Diocesan Structure

A typical local, or diocesan, structure is shown in figure 3-2.[11] In an individual diocese the bishop, or ordinary (the title for a bishop who has ordinary authority over a diocese), possesses ultimate and sole authority. All other functionaries in a diocese derive their authority from him. When a bishop dies or leaves a diocese, the vicar general, the priests' senate, and the pastoral council go out of existence. They may later be called into existence at the discretion of the new bishop but he does not have to call them back (in a

Figure 3-2. Diocesan Organization Structure

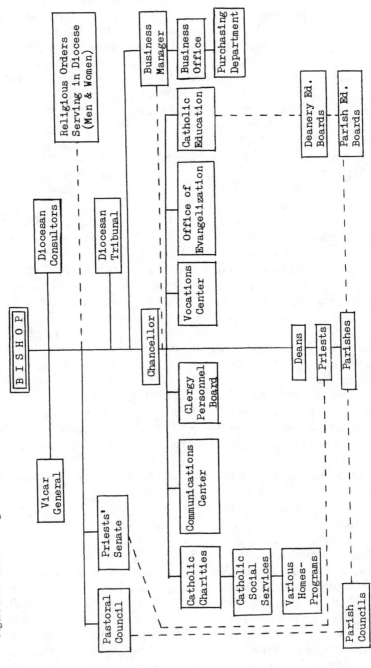

diocese in which a priests' senate or pastoral council has been functioning effectively for years it is, however, unlikely that a new bishop will eliminate them).

The priests' senate and pastoral council are consultative bodies elected by the priests and the parishes (through the parish councils) respectively. The priests' senate is made up entirely of diocesan priests (priests with appointments in the diocese) while the pastoral council is composed of diocesan priests, lay people, and religious men and women (men and women serving in religious orders). The priests' senate consults with the bishop about concerns of the priests (e.g., recruitment, pay, pensions, retirement, etc.) while the pastoral council consults with the bishop on concerns of the laity (which may, and often do, include human interest and political issues). Once again it is important to note, its primary job is advising but not instructing the bishop. Both pastoral councils and priests' senates ultimately owe their existence to the pastoral emphasis of Vatican II which encourages bishops to consult with their priests and their "flock." With the new promulgation of canon law both have become canon law structures. However, while priests' senates have been successfully established in virtually all U.S. dioceses, pastoral councils have not caught on very quickly. Only 56 percent of U.S. dioceses surveyed have pastoral councils. The Archdiocese of Indianapolis does not presently have one although most of the prelates interviewed seem confident that one will be established in the future.

The vicar general is a sort of "assistant bishop" or, as one cleric suggested to the author, the bishop's alter ego. When a diocese has an auxiliary bishop (a bishop who does not have ordinary authority but, rather, assists the ordinary in running the diocese) he is automatically appointed vicar general. (Another bishop who assists an ordinary is called a coadjutor bishop. This position is similar to that of the auxiliary bishop except that a coadjutor bishop also has the right to succeed the ordinary. Where there is a coadjutor bishop he is automatically appointed vicar general.)

Diocesan consultors are priests who provide advice and information to the bishop. With the relatively recent development of the priests' senate and other advisory groups these positions are rapidly becoming outmoded and no longer exist effectively in many dioceses.

The diocesan tribunal, like the Roman and regional tribunals, is essentially a court which interprets canon law. In Indianapolis and other dioceses this has come to be called the marriage tribunal as virtually all cases brought to it today involve requests for annulment of marriages.

Religious orders are, in figure 3-2, linked to the bishop with a dotted line because they are not part of the diocese. They have their own hierarchical reporting system (superiors, abbots, etc.) and only consult with the bishop when offering their services (teaching, nursing, etc.) within the bishop's diocese. A bishop has no direct authority over religious orders, which may supply many important services. Nevertheless, a bishop may choose to have a troublesome order banned from work in his diocese.

The administrative structure of a diocese is divided into two major areas: the business office and the chancery. The business office, which became a juridical structure with the new canon law, is primarily responsible for oversight of financial issues. The chancery, under direction of the chancellor (in some dioceses this position may have a different title, such as vicar for administration), is primarily concerned with handling diocesan programs. While technically the chancellor has nothing to do with temporalities and the business administrator nothing to do with spiritual concerns, in reality these two areas often overlap.

The offices listed as directly under the control of the chancellor are, as are the congregations in the Vatican, essentially staff departments. Dependent on the diocese, there may be a greater or smaller number or the offices may be different. The ones shown here, however, are those which interview and questionnaire data indicate are fairly typical of U.S. dioceses. Some of these offices enjoy line authority over specific programs (e.g., the Office of Catholic Social Services oversees operation of counseling programs). Some, such as education and social services, have complex structures of their own including governing boards.

Deans are priests who act as the bishop's representative in smaller geographical segments of the diocese called deaneries (some dioceses refer to these men as area vicars). The deans may check the books of individual parishes and perform some functions on short notice when the bishop cannot attend. The deans are also responsible for keeping the bishop informed in general of events occurring in the deanery.

The individual priests are responsible to minister to the parishes (or, in a few cases, carry out some special ministry). The priest in charge of a parish has ordinary authority in that parish just as a bishop has ordinary authority in a diocese. Junior priests in the parish must defer to him. In the Catholic church, unlike many Protestant denominations, parishes are laid out geographically—people who reside in the confines of a particular parish are expected to attend the church in that parish.

Many parishes have parish councils and parish boards of education. The parish council is elected by the members of the parish. The pastor and assistant pastors, chairperson of the parish board of education, and chairperson of the women's guild are included as ex-officio members. If the diocese has a pastoral council, members are usually chosen by the parish councils. The priests' senate is elected by the diocesan priests.

The parish board of education is also chosen by members of the parish. Parish boards then choose representatives to deanery boards of education and the deanery boards in turn select representatives to the diocesan board of education.

In this research we will also be looking closely at the Board of Catholic Social Services. This board is self-electing. Members of the board nominate and vote on replacements for members when their terms expire.

In the Archdiocese of Indianapolis funding comes from four major sources. First, assessments to the parishes make up about 46 percent of budget funds. These assessments are arbitrarily set based on various factors, the main one being the ability to pay. The second source of funds is the Archbishop's Annual Appeal which provides about 32 percent of budget funds. This is an annual drive which solicits funds directly from parishioners. About one-half of U.S. dioceses have some sort of appeal drive. Restricted funds make up about four percent of budget funds. These are gifts which are given by donors who request that they be used for a specific purpose. Fees and miscellaneous income are the fourth source of diocesan funds, providing about 18 percent of the budget. The largest source of income in this category is interest. Included here also are certain fees charged for services (e.g., fees charged by Catholic social service agencies based on the clients' ability to pay).

While sources of income and their importance do vary from diocese to diocese, interview and survey data give the impression that, at least within the U.S., the Indianapolis pattern is fairly typical. The major sources of funds are the parishes and parishioners. The nature of investments may be different. Indianapolis, for example, avoids investment in equities while other dioceses do invest in these but most dioceses surveyed indicated that this provided a very small portion of their incomes.

Finally, some of the diocesan offices have additional sources of income outside of the diocese's budget. The Board of Catholic Social Services in Indianapolis, for example, receives more than half of its funding from the United Way. While the Office of Education is funded by the archdiocese, Catholic schools receive their funding from individual parishes and tuition fees.

Prelates and Their Titles

Before moving on, the formal relationship among cardinals, archbishops, bishops, and monsignors should be explained briefly. "Monsignor" is a title granted by Rome to a priest in recognition of exceptional service. It carries no special weight or privileges beyond that normally associated with an honor and long service.

A bishop and archbishop nominally enjoy the same rank and have absolute authority over their respective dioceses (an archbishop cannot interfere with a bishop in the running of his diocese). An archbishop, also called a metropolitan because he has authority in a metropolitan see or archdiocese, is responsible, however, for calling and presiding over meetings of the province. In the United States provinces usually follow state borders and are made up of several dioceses. The Province of Indiana, for example, is made up of the Archdiocese of Indianapolis and the Dioceses of Lafayette, Gary, Evansville, and Fort Wayne-South Bend. An archbishop cannot force a bishop to action; however, a bishop who wants to advance in the church will usually participate in meetings of the province.

A cardinal has no authority over bishops or archbishops. Cardinal is, most simply, the title given to those who enjoy the privilege of electing the pope. In the past a cardinal was not always a priest and, while it is apparently still possible for someone who is not a priest to be appointed cardinal, this doesn't actually happen today. In the United States cardinals are appointed to primacial sees—dioceses, such as Baltimore, which were established early in U.S. history. Very large dioceses, such as Chicago (which was originally part of the Diocese of Vincennes and is not, therefore, considered a primacial see), often become the seats of cardinals as well.

4

Resource Dependence and the Roman Catholic Church

Precisely because of its traditional bureaucratic nature and flavor of being a total institution...the Roman Catholic church allows the investigation of various issues in organizational behavior.
—Douglas T. Hall and Benjamin Schneider

...all the large-scale religious organizations exhibit a characteristic similarity of cultural accommodation to the secular society.
—Joseph H. Fichter

There is a good deal of evidence that, as highlighted in the above quotations, religious organizations act in many ways like secular organizations. Chapter 2 in particular highlights the close relationships between events in the secular environment and in the Catholic church. The interdependence of the church and its environment suggests that valuable insights into the operations and organization of the Catholic church can be gained by applying a resource dependence approach to the study of local units (dioceses) of the Catholic church.

The primary focus of this study is the Archdiocese of Indianapolis. This unit was chosen for two reasons. First, a unit of the church is needed which is large enough to have, potentially, significant influence in an area but which is not so large as to be impossible to study. A parish is too small because it enjoys very little influence over political and economic events in a significant area. A larger unit of the church, such as the Archdiocese of Chicago, may enjoy power on a national scale but is too big and complex to be studied adequately. An institutional study of a medium-sized diocese is, therefore, determined to be the best approach for this research.

The second reason for choosing the Archdiocese of Indianapolis is accessibility. A major purpose of the study is to test the application of the resource dependence model to a religious group. A logical first step is to find an accessible unit which might also be fairly representative of other units. This is done using the Archdiocese of Indianapolis. Additionally, the author was affiliated with a large institution within the geographic area of the diocese at the time of the study. As a result the author could exploit the many connections existing between members of this institution and members of the archdiocese's administrative structure, making the archdiocese more accessible.

In this study the relationship of the diocese with two major constituencies, the local community and the Vatican, will be assessed. The resource dependence model, introduced in chapter 1, will be the primary vehicle used to assess these relationships.

Rationale for the Study

Having presented an overview of the formal structure of the church in chapter 3 we now begin to consider how the church adapts to pressures, both internal and external, placed on it. This study is primarily concerned with real world adjustments which are made by local (diocesan) church units.

Any organization makes adjustments in order to deal with unique developments, or contingencies, in its external and internal environment. In the cases of business and government organizations and certain nonprofit groups such as hospitals these adjustments are the subject of a great deal of study. The activities, influences, and structures of religious organizations have not, however, received similar attention.

Need for Study of Religious Organizations

This study is based on the premise that religious organizations, and specifically the Roman Catholic church, have enough in common with secular organizations to allow for similar approaches to study of both. At the same time, significant differences exist, creating a need for separate studies focusing on religious groups.

A clear area of difference, for example, exists in the area of goals and direction.[1] The church is other-world directed and its official (public) goals are focused on salvation. Secular organizations are this-world directed and their goals are generally focused on survival, if not profitability. A conceivable outcome of this difference, specifically with respect to resource dependence theory, may be a change in the intensity of concern over supplies of resources and, therefore, differences in the number and nature of linkages formed.

In terms of formal organization structure there are clear similarities and differences. One can speak of the church using terms from management and military studies such as hierarchy of authority, line and staff functions, division of labor, and task specialization. The Vatican is a temporal government as well as a spiritual one. On the other hand, hierarchical relationships are viewed as more collegial than in many temporal organizations while concurrently being, in some ways, more autocratic as well (e.g., the absolute authority of a bishop in his diocese who, at the same time, is officially on a par with other bishops, archbishops, cardinals, and even the pope).

These differences make the church somewhat unique as an organization and, therefore, worth studying. At the same time, many authors who have studied the church as an organization have identified trends and processes that frequently duplicate those of temporal groups. Warwick, for example, links the increasing centralization of the Catholic church (which led to the declaration of papal infallibility in 1870) to an increase in the number of external threats.[2] O'Dea argues that the growing tendency of people to identify with their jobs in Western, industrialized countries required an organizational reaction (Vatican II) on the part of the church. He also notes the enormous institutional resistance (common to most large organizations) which had to be overcome first.[3]

Metz sees the church as being in competition with other organizations, both religious and temporal, and argues that there is increasing need for the church to respond more efficiently to "consumer" needs.[4] Both Nichols and Vaskovics also reflect a growing need for the church to be responsive to the environment. Much of Nichols' book, *The Pope's Divisions*, concentrates on the roles played by external forces in shaping the character of today's Catholic church.[5] Vaskovics also shows that churches must rely on the environment and other organizations if they are to survive.[6]

Value of This Study

This study extends the focus on relationships between the church and its environment. Going beyond a concentration on the impact that parishioners (or the need for them) may have, it will expand the focus to include the church's quest for financial and nonparishioner (external community) support. The resource dependence approach will be used to impose rigor and continuity on the research. This is, in short, a study of the Roman Catholic church from a management perspective performed by an "outsider," or non-Catholic. This combination, along with the focus on greater methodological rigor, contributes to the uniqueness of the particular research.

Because the resource dependence approach has been tested largely by studying composition of management and advisory boards (e.g., boards of directors) this approach will be used here.[7] Advisory boards are frequently used to reduce external uncertainty for a particular organization. This is done by appointing as members individuals with connections to other organizations critical to the focal organization (often suppliers of critical inputs).[8] Given the assumption (explained earlier) that religious organizations can be studied using guidelines developed in research on temporal groups we would expect that advisory boards in the diocese studied will exhibit characteristics similar to those of boards in other organizations. That is, they will be composed largely of individuals who represent organizations that are critical suppliers of the diocese. In this study our primary focus will be on organizations that provide funding for diocesan programs. This will allow more precise empirical testing. However, suppliers of other resources will not be ignored and will be discussed as appropriate.

In moving from tests using business and government advisory boards to study of religious boards a major problem is encountered. Most secular testing has focused on centrally located advisory boards which usually exercise formal authority (e.g., a corporate board of directors). But, as can be seen in chapter 3, no board exists in a diocese in exactly the same capacity. The bishop formally possesses all authority in a diocese and, as a result, all boards are merely advisory. Additionally, it is difficult to find a board central in a diocesan structure which exists in most U.S. dioceses at the present time. The priests' senate is a possibility but, being composed entirely of priests, will not include individuals who are members of other organizations and, therefore, could best represent suppliers. The pastoral council is not found widely enough and has not been in place long enough in most dioceses to be useful.

In an effort to solve this problem two boards were identified which do appear to exist in most dioceses, are long established, and, while not in a central position, are located well up in the hierarchy. These are the Diocesan Board of Education and the Board of Catholic Social Services. These two boards will, therefore, be the focus of this study.

Links with the Local Community

It is expected that members of these boards will be selected largely for their connections to other important organizations rather than for their functional or administrative abilities. Board composition should change as resource providers change, more recently appointed members reflecting more accurately the current needs of the diocese (the manner in which board members are selected is discussed in the section of chapter 3 on diocesan structure).

It is also expected that the size of these advisory boards will reflect economic conditions (i.e., the difficulty of obtaining financial support). When economic conditions are bad (e.g., recession) it is expected that board size will increase in order to provide more links to potential sources of funding. Additionally, outside membership (nonchurch employees) on boards will increase more than inside membership (e.g., priests, nuns) because outside members have a greater potential for providing supplier links. These assumptions about size are based on findings of a 1972 study which concluded that "the size of the board . . . was related to the organization's need for linkage to the environment."[9]

The Vatican as a Resource Provider

Because Rome does not provide or control funding for diocesan programs (nor, apparently, many other critical resources) it is expected that the Vatican will have very limited contact with the diocese and, realistically, very limited discretion with respect to such things as the appointment of diocesan prelates. Rome may, in fact, be quite dependent on individual dioceses for advice and suggestions on the appointment of local prelates.

The findings of this resource dependence study combined with the more formal development of church structure presented earlier, will, potentially, contribute to a much richer understanding of the Roman Catholic church as an important organization in the environment confronting all of us. Additionally, if a research approach can be used to study both temporal and spiritual organizations, then it may be hoped that lessons learned about management in one organization, such as the Catholic church, may be useful in more effectively managing others.

Research Methods

Sources of Data

Three types of data were collected in studying the Archdiocese of Indianapolis: questionnaire, interview, and archival. Questionnaires were sent to each individual who had served on either the Diocesan Board of Education or the Board of Catholic Social Services from 1965 through 1982. The return rate of these was extremely good. In the case of the Board of Education 62 out of 88 sent were returned, a 70.4 percent response rate. In the case of the Board of Catholic Social Services, 55 of 101 were returned, a response rate of 54.4 percent. The overall response rate was, therefore, 117 of 189 sent or 61.9 percent. The rate is somewhat underestimated because 20 of the 189 sent were returned undeliverable due to people having moved since serving their terms on the board.

The questionnaire was very short and structured so as to allow a limited number of possible responses in most cases. As will be described in more detail shortly, the responses were coded, in many cases, to allow for empirical analysis.

Open-ended interviews provided a second source of information on the archdiocese. In conjunction with the questionnaire sent to current and past board members, some of the current employees of both boards were interviewed in an effort to develop a better understanding of the functions and structures of both agencies. Interviews were conducted both during the preparation of the questionnaire as well as after the questionnaire had been returned and analyzed.

Interviews were also conducted with the archbishop, the vicar general, the chancellor, the business manager, eight of the twelve prelates (those with the title monsignor; four of the prelates and the retired archbishop were unavailable for reasons of health), the director of the Indiana Catholic Conference (a legislative lobbying group), and the provincial of the Sisters of Providence. These interviews were open-ended and some of those listed resulted from the suggestions of others who were interviewed early in the study. The primary purpose of these interviews was to develop a better understanding of the general structure and operations of a diocese. They also provide information on the amount of diocesan contact with other church organizations and with Rome. Included in those interviewed were both those serving primarily as parish priests as well as those serving functions in the diocesan hierarchy. The one group that is not represented is younger priests. This may be a drawback in the sense that it might be expected that younger priests would be more active in local community issues, a perspective which often seemed to be less important to many, though certainly not all, of those interviewed. (Because those interviewed were promised anonymity specific contents of the interviews are not recorded.)

The third type of data collected was archival. This includes data on attendance at board meetings and on size and composition of the administrative boards. In this way it was possible to obtain personal profiles on board members which were used to substantiate findings of the questionnaire. Literature describing the functions of each board, its revenues and expenses, and such things as rules for selection of the boards was also acquired. The minutes of the priests' senate and additional information acquired from the archdiocesan archives at St. Mary-of-the-Woods College in Terre Haute, Indiana, provided background information on the history of the diocese and problems which it has confronted. The archdiocesan newspaper, *The Criterion*, was also used to acquire some information on diocesan finances and history. Finally, archival data provided much of the information which was used for independent variables in the analysis. This information included Catholic school enrollments and the number of clients of Catholic social services. Unemployment data for the area of the archdiocese, the city of Indianapolis, and the state of Indiana provided measures of the state of the economy during much of the period of this study. The condition of the economy, as noted earlier, is presumed to have an impact on the size and composition of the two boards.

Measures of the Variables

Wherever possible, data collected were quantified and analyzed empirically. Frequently information received from the questionnaires was coded in such a way as to facilitate empirical analysis.

In studying board composition the author was concerned with measuring two things: 1) the qualifications of those serving on a board, and 2) the occupational prestige of board members. Qualifications of those serving on a board were assessed based on three items: 1) whether or not the individual had experience in the function supervised by the board; 2) the level of formal education completed by the board member; and 3) the nature of that education, specifically, was it in the function supervised by the board served on? Information provided in answers to the questions was coded to represent different levels of experience and education. Occupational prestige of board members was calculated using Duncan's socioeconomic index.[10]

Information on board size and outside membership was collected from archival data provided by the Diocesan Board of Education and by the Board of Catholic Social Services. Records of board memberships had been maintained for many of the years studied (1974-1981) and, as a result, these figures could be determined with relative ease. Minor difficulties were encountered with the Board of Education in that information on the occupations of members (used to identify inside versus outside members) was not always kept for earlier years. This problem was overcome through interviews with board employees (long-time employees were often able to identify priests or nuns who had served on past boards who were then categorized as inside members). Past and current issues of the diocese's published directory also helped to identify members of the board who were church employees. All others were then assumed to be outside members (board members who were not employed by the church). Ex-officio members of the board are included in the figures because, while they may not have a vote on board issues, they can still serve as links to groups in the environment, which is the focus of this research. If an ex-officio appointment is clearly a formality, however, such as the inclusion of the archbishop as an ex-officio member of the Board of Social Services, he or she is not included in the count. It is assumed that, in such a situation, the individual does not have close enough contact with the board to provide an important link. On the other hand, an ex-officio member, such as the diocesan superintendent of schools who sits on the Board of Education, is expected to be actively involved in board meetings and, therefore, is counted.

Three area unemployment figures are computed as measures of economic health for the period studied. Unemployment figures are collected for each county in the area of the archdiocese and a figure for "archdiocesan unemployment" is computed. Because this figure expresses employment conditions over the exact territory covered by the archdiocese, this variable is expected to bear the closest relationship to board size. It became clear, however, after conducting interviews, that the archdiocese is dominated by the city of Indianapolis and, therefore, city employment figures are also collected and correlated with board size and outside membership. Finally, unemployment rates for the state of Indiana are also used in this study. This is done because state figures are often the most publicized during difficult economic times. If we assume that board size is related to economic upturns and downturns then it is conceivable that the size will vary with those indicators that are in the news, rather than with conditions in a specific area which are harder to obtain and, therefore, probably given less attention by diocesan administrators.

In measuring unemployment rates no attempt is made to assess what should be considered a high or low rate. Rather, it is assumed that if unemployment is falling then economic times are good. On the other hand, if unemployment is rising then the area is facing more difficult economic times and, according to the predictions of this study, board size and outside membership should also increase. Unfortunately, data on unemployment for the areas studied are only available for eight of the eighteen years studied (1974-1981). As a result of this small sample, correlations computed are often insignificant even though many are in the direction indicated or suggest other interesting relationships.

Data on the number of clients served (school enrollments for the Board of Education) are obtained primarily from the records kept by the boards studied. School enrollment figures are available for the period from 1970 through the present. However, figures on clients served by Catholic Social Services are only available beginning in 1975. Because of this, data on social services expenses are obtained for the entire period (1965-1981) and used as a coincident indicator of task size. Data on the number of special religious instruction students (students enrolled in community schools but taking additional religious studies courses through the diocesan schools) are obtained from *The Official Catholic Directory* published by P. J. Kenedy & Sons of New York. All of this information is used as an indicator of the sizes of the constituencies and, therefore, the task sizes of the respective boards.

Attendance at board meetings is taken directly from the minutes of the respective boards for the years studied. In a few cases specific meeting minutes are missing; however, for both boards at least 10 years of substantially complete data are available.

Resources provided by Rome and number of contacts with Rome are both assessed through interview data. Some additional information is obtained from recent issues of the diocesan newspaper. Because of the very descriptive nature of the interviews this data cannot be coded or quantified.

To assess the number of board links to outside organizations the number of organizations listed by each respondent to the survey are simply counted and totalled. To assess the nature of links each organization is assigned a code based on a scheme developed by the author. These codes are used in much the same way that the socioeconomic ratings are used to assess board member prestige. Each organization listed by respondents is assigned a unique number so that the number of links with a specific organization can be counted easily using a computer. We are, however, most interested in assessing the general types of links. For this reason eight major categories are set up which can be accessed easily (these categories are, basically: church units, government and educational units, law firms, business firms, financial businesses, medical and retirement care units, community service groups, and social clubs).

This completes the list of variables studied in the diocesan research. Because this is an exploratory study seeking merely to determine if predicted relationships do appear to exist, frequencies and correlations are the primary types of statistics computed and used in the analysis. In most cases the purpose is not strict empirical testing of hypotheses but, rather, a more descriptive analysis of relationships which are not always quantifiable. It is hoped that this more descriptive approach will provide the desired insight both into the usefulness of resource dependence theory in studies of religious groups and into the management and activities of the Catholic church.

5

Linking the Religious to the Secular: Findings of the Study

I pray not that thou shouldest take them out of the world, but that thou shouldest keep them from evil.
—John 18:15 (King James Bible)

Christ clearly foresaw that his followers would continue to exist within a threatening and frequently hostile environment. This book is premised on the concept that those followers, as represented for purposes of study by the Roman Catholic organization, have dealt with that hostility, at least in part, by using methods common to many different groups, whether secular or religious. Chapter 2 considered the existence and consequences of efforts by the church to exert influence in nonreligious matters, specifically in economic affairs. This chapter attempts to uncover some of the channels which have been developed in an effort to make influence attempts more effective in reducing uncertainty (or hostility) in the secular world.

This particular study is focused on the Archdiocese of Indianapolis, a unit of the Catholic church responsible for the religious lives of roughly 200,000 parishioners. The archdiocese has been quite active in the larger community as is evidenced by the archbishop's many commitments and speaking engagements (including participation in the opening ceremonies of at least one Indianapolis 500 race).

As discussed in chapter 4, the empirical part of this study concentrates primarily on the role of advisory boards as linking devices. This is done because other research has suggested that boards (specifically boards of directors) are a very important linkage mechanism in the business community. The results of this focus will indicate if boards are useful in the same way to this religious unit and, if so, to what degree. Study of these boards, along with descriptive data on other aspects of the diocese's structure, also provides unique insights regarding the administration and power structure in this church unit. Following this analysis, chapter 6 will discuss the results of a subsequent attempt to apply knowledge gained in this case study to study of Catholic dioceses nationwide.

Findings of the Combined Study of the Board of Catholic Education and the Board of Catholic Social Services

Experience and Expertise

It is expected that advisory boards will be composed largely of individuals who can form links with the environment rather than of experts in the task supervised. To study this, current and past board members were asked to respond to questions regarding any experience they might have had in the function supervised (e.g., a member of the board of education might have worked as a teacher for several years). Additionally, respondents were asked about college degrees and other training they had as a means of assessing expertise in the task supervised. Approximately 37 percent of all respondents indicated they had some sort of experience in the area of concern of the board on which they served. A majority of board members did not, therefore, have experience related to board tasks, as was predicted.

The results on the expertise question were even more striking. Of all the degrees earned by current or past board members, only 9 percent of those held by social services board members and 20 percent of those held by education board members were in the respective fields supervised. These tendencies were also found in the archival data. Post-survey interviews with social services officers indicated that in upcoming elections members were being sought who could provide good links with the United Way, an important source of funding. While these results do not rule out the possibility that some board members are chosen for their functional ability, it is clear that some significant consideration is given to "supplier" links.

Occupational Prestige

The church's pattern of critical resource suppliers should also be reflected in board composition. To measure board composition Duncan's measure of occupational prestige was used.[1] This ranges occupations from a low score of "2" to a high score of "96." Unemployment figures over time were used as indicators of the economic climate. It was expected that the boards would seek out more prestigious members during periods of economic hardship (high unemployment) if a major concern is linkage. Such a result would parallel the findings of a study of privately funded hospitals concerning board prestige.[2] If, as would seem logical, high prestige can be used as an approximation for potential to wield influence, then, in an organization which is reliant on private funding, it makes sense to expect that the prestige of members would rise during periods of economic stress to offset greater uncertainty in the supply of funding. At the same time deviation in the prestige ratings would be low because only prestigious members would be desired. If, on the other hand, the boards do in fact represent Catholic parishioners (a socially diverse group) rather than functioning to secure resources, then there should be high variance in the socioeconomic status of board members.

In the cases of both boards the average prestige scores do not vary much from year to year. Social services scores on Duncan's scale ranged from an average of 64 to 74 over a 17-year period; education scores ranged from an average of 51 to 72 over the same period (see table 5-1). In both cases high prestige occupations were, in fact, somewhat over-represented. In the case of the Board of Catholic Social Services there was little variance (overall standard deviation = 20); business executives were dominant and lawyers and college professors appeared frequently. There seemed to be a slight increase over time in the number of attorneys and executives. The relatively high prestige ratings (overall mean = 68), which changed little over time, and the over-representation of attorneys and executives on the Board of Social Services provide tentative support for the predictions. It should be noted that on the Board of Social Services, which does a great deal of family counseling, interviews indicated that attorneys can represent an important nonmonetary resource. The type of service provided by this agency does, apparently, carry some risk that legal action may be taken against the agency.

While these general trends with respect to prestige were as expected, no significant relationship was found, however, between the unemployment figures and prestige scores. None of the correlations of the prestige scores of newly appointed members with three different measures of unemployment, shown in table 5-2, were significant ($p < .05$). This was true even when the dependent variables (the new member prestige scores) were lagged to attempt to account for possible recognition, decision, and implementation delays in the appointment of new members.

Board Size and Outside Membership

To test the prediction that board size and outside membership would increase in times of economic hardship, correlational analyses were again used. In this case the three measures of unemployment shown in table 5-2 were correlated with board sizes and outside memberships. The dependent variables, in this test the board size measures, were again lagged in an attempt to consider the effects of possible delays in reacting to economic changes. The board size measures are also correlated with measures of the task size for each board to

Table 5-1. Social Services and Education Prestige Scores

Year	Social Services Averages	Social Services Standard Deviations	Education Averages	Education Standard Deviations
1965	65.7	19.117	72.2	20.253
1966	70.2	17.398	70.4	18.243
1967	68.3	14.648	68.8	16.762
1968	72.8	16.827	64.1	13.791
1969	74.0	15.910	67.2	13.841
1970	66.8	26.286	64.4	13.538
1971	67.0	24.580	64.4	16.712
1972	70.9	16.538	61.5	17.550
1973	70.9	16.538	63.3	17.313
1974	67.1	15.757	60.1	15.431
1975	69.1	16.671	57.1	18.871
1976	69.4	18.300	51.0	13.754
1977	67.1	19.116	58.6	14.193
1978	66.6	18.429	60.4	13.959
1979	64.3	18.272	60.6	13.924
1980	66.6	19.772	53.3	18.201
1981	67.2	19.019	55.7	19.802
1982	67.6	21.295	54.4	19.712

Table 5-2. Correlations of New Member Prestige Ratings with
Unemployment Data

	Metropolitan Area Unemployment	Diocesan Area Unemployment	State Area Unemployment
Social Services New Member Prestige	.4289	.1902	−.0937
Education New Member Prestige	.4705	−.0482	−.1957
Social Services NMP Lagged 1 Year	.2056	−.5224	−.4944
Education NMP Lagged 1 Year	.4255	−.3138	−.3441
Social Services NMP Lagged 2 Years	.1742	−.2823	.3694
Education NMP Lagged 2 Years	.3985	.7107	.1892

determine if task size is related to board size (little or no relationship is predicted). Task size is assessed using the number of students enrolled in Catholic schools (for the Board of Education) and the number of clients of Catholic Social Services (for the Board of Social Services).

These correlations are shown in table 5-3. It can be seen that no significant relationships emerged that were in the direction predicted. In fact, significant and strong negative correlations were found between the three unemployment variables and the measure of social services outside membership for both unlagged data and data lagged one year. This would indicate that Board of Social Services outside membership decreased during economic downturns, just the opposite of the relationship predicted. On the other hand high correlations were found for Board of Education outside membership with unemployment variables in the unlagged tests and for tests lagged two years, but in all cases the correlations were not significant. This was also true for the comparison of Board of Social Services size with the economic data when a two year lag was introduced. None of the correlations of Board of Education size with the economic data were significant; once again in some cases the associations were in a direction opposite to that predicted. The results, therefore, do not support the predictions with respect to the relationship between size and unemployment or between outside membership and unemployment.

The majority of correlations in table 5-3 on the task size measures are not significant and many are often quite low. This is as expected given the assumption that boards do not function in a predominantly supervisory role. However, the Board of Social Services membership size does produce a very high and significant correlation with the task size measure when the membership figures are lagged two years (r = .8538). A high figure (though not significant) is also obtained when social services membership lagged only one year is compared to task size data. These findings are clearly contrary to expectations. It is also interesting to note that all three tests of the relationship between Board of Education outside membership size and task size produce significant but negative correlations. While overall membership figures for education are, as expected, unrelated to task size, it appears that outside membership actually *decreases* when task size increases. More specifically, in the archdiocese studied, as Catholic school enrollments fell, outside board membership grew. This may indicate an effort to seek other sources of support as the single most important source of finances—tuition fees—shrinks. If so, this pattern would still fit predictions. Therefore, while there apparently is a relationship between task size and outside membership in the case of the Board of Education, that relationship may be directed at replacing a dwindling source of support. On the other hand, these unexpected correlations may simply indicate the existence of trends in enrollments and

Table 5-3.   Board Membership with Unemployment Data Correlations

Social Services	Metro. Area Unemp.	Dioc. Area Unemp.	State Area Unemp.	Task‡ Size Measure
Membership	-.3915	-.4493	-.5416	-.0710
Membership Lagged 1 Year	-.2884	-.2921	-.1382	.6024
Membership Lagged 2 Years	.4018	.3808	.5524	.8538*
Outside Membership	-.6222*	-.6574*	-.7951†	-.6499
Outside Membership Lagged 1 Year	-.7802*	-.7800*	-.6915*	-.1525
Outside Membership Lagged 2 Years	-.2775	-.2892	-.0684	.3723
Education				
Membership	-.2793	-.2696	-.3082	.0082
Membership Lagged 1 Year	-.3562	-.4238	-.4162	.0314
Membership Lagged 2 Years	.0134	.1127	.2883	-.0833
Outside Membership	.4414	.4129	.3485	-.6321*
Outside Membership Lagged 1 Year	-.0847	-.1341	-.0854	-.7887*
Outside Membership Lagged 2 Years	.5445	.5580	.6787	-.7840*

*p < .05
†p < .01
‡Education Students or Social Service Clients

recruiting which are, in fact, unrelated in the case studied. In any event, these findings clearly do not indicate that task size is an important consideration in the sense that members of the Board of Education are selected to cope with a growing or shrinking work load.

The results of these correlations testing the relationships of board size and outside membership to task size and economic climate are mixed. There is no support for the expectation that size and outside membership will be related to economic conditions (and specifically unemployment) in the way predicted. There is, in fact, some indication that the size of the Board of Social Services is related to the size of its task. In the case of the Board of Education, however, there is some support for the prediction that board size will be unrelated to task size. The unexpected negative correlations may, in this case, even suggest a pattern which can be explained from a resource dependence perspective.

Unpredicted Differences between Boards

In designing this research no attempt was made to predict differences between the Board of Catholic Education and the Board of Catholic Social Services; both were expected to serve as linking devices for the entire diocese in lieu of a more central or "corporate" board. In testing the initial predictions, however, there was some evidence that board membership was rather closely related to the specific concerns of the individual boards rather than those of the diocese as a whole. Specifically, funding sources differ greatly, resulting in differences in the nature of the task environments of the two boards. The Board of Education is funded primarily with money allocated by the diocese. Catholic schools are funded primarily by tuition fees and by assessments from the parishes, each source accounting for approximately 40 percent of the school budgets. Elementary schools tend to be connected with individual parishes and are more heavily subsidized by parish assessments than are high schools, whose funding is controlled by the deanery (or district) boards.

The Board of Social Services, on the other hand, receives a great deal of its funding from the United Way and from government agencies. A pamphlet highlighting agency activities showed sources of income for 1980 to be dominated by agencies other than the church (93 percent provided by nonchurch sources). Interviews indicate that this breakdown is typical for agency funding in the past several years and for the funding of social services in other dioceses nationally.

Looking at the differences in funding sources, the Board of Education is considerably less dependent on outside funding than is the Board of Social Services. Its structure should therefore be influenced less by the need for resources from outside the church organization.

According to resource dependence theory one place where these differences should be reflected is in the characteristics (or qualifications) of people selected to serve on these boards. For this reason discriminant analysis is used to attempt to develop a function which might predict membership on each board using board member characteristics. Discriminant analysis is used rather than regression because the dependent variable, board membership, is categorical rather than continuous. Resource dependence theory leads us to expect that several of the discriminating variables selected for inclusion in the function should be related to the differences in funding sources of the two boards. Variables which are run in the discriminant analysis include the board member's sex, socioeconomic status, age, work experience, educational background, number of memberships in Catholic and non-Catholic organizations, and the number of positions held on the governing boards of other Catholic and non-Catholic organizations.

The Discriminant Function

Of the above items five are included in the discriminant function (table 5-4). Other variables do not enter the equation because their tolerance level is too low. The variables with the strongest coefficients are the number of positions on non-Catholic governing boards and the individual's age, followed by the number of positions on Catholic organizations' governing boards and memberships in Catholic organizations (both inversely related) and, finally, sex.

Table 5-4.   Results of Discriminant Analysis

Variables Included in the Discriminant Function	Standardized Discriminant Function Coefficients
Sex (0 = Male, 1 = Female)	.36234
Positions on Catholic Governing Boards	-.42089
Positions on Non-Catholic Governing Boards	.73627
Memberships on Catholic Organizations	-.39276
Age	.64559

Subgroup Classification

The group centroids for the two subgroups are shown in table 5-5. The results show that members of the Board of Social Services tend to be characterized by a positive score on the function, while those on the Board of Education tend to receive a negative score. This indicates that members of the Board of Social Services tend to be active on the governing boards of non-Catholic organizations while being poorly represented in Catholic organizations or on their governing boards. They also tend to be older individuals and are relatively more likely to be female. Board of Education members reflect the mirror opposite of Board of Social Services members.

Table 5-5.   Group Centroids

Group 1: Board of Catholic Social Services	.50443
Group 2: Board of Catholic Education	-.37168

It was predicted, in carrying out the discriminant analysis, that the differences in funding sources would be reflected in the structure of a discriminant function which is based on member characteristics. This prediction is clearly correct. Three of the variables selected for inclusion in the function, those having to do with organization or board memberships, are direct measures of personal linkages with other organizations which might supply funding. With respect to these variables members of the Board of Social Services tend to be active in secular organizations while, conversely, members of the Board of Education are more active in church groups. This is clearly logical given the sources of funding if, as expected, an important concern in selecting board members is their ability to provide linkages with important sources of funding.

The importance of age in the function is a bit of a surprise. It may be that older members are preferred on the Board of Social Services because they are likely to hold more powerful positions in other organizations as a result of longevity. This would make some sense, given social services' heavy reliance on outside funding. The Board of Education, on the other hand, may simply have trouble locating volunteers other than those in the age group that would have children in school and, therefore, be most interested in the board's activities.

Discussion of Discriminant Analysis

The results of the discriminant analysis do support the expectation that board member characteristics will differ in ways that reflect differences in sources of funding. Members of the Board of Social Services tend to have many more ties to outside organizations than do members of the Board of Education. This is logical if, as suggested by the resource dependence model, individuals on governing boards are, to a great extent, chosen for their ability to provide links to important suppliers of resources. The high level of activity by Board of Education members in other church groups probably also reflects, to some extent, their method of election. Those who are most active in church activities are most likely to be nominated by other parishioners.

Because the specific organizations in which board members are active are not identified in this analysis it is possible that while the type of organizations on which members are active fit expectations, the actual organizations which are linked to the respective boards by their members are not, in fact, suppliers of funding. Unstructured, posthoc interviews with some of the members of the Board of Social Services did, however, reveal a large number of links to specific funding sources.

The discriminant function which was developed in this analysis was only able to accurately predict 59 percent of the cases (see tables 5-6 and 5-7). It would appear that while the expected relationships between sources of funding and board membership are evident, more discriminating variables could be developed. An important consideration might be the individual's status in the organization which is being linked to the board. Clearly the categories of organizations could be delineated beyond the simple Catholic/non-Catholic dichotomy which was used.

Table 5-6.   Characteristics of Function

Eigenvalue	.19
Percent of Variance	100
Canonical Correlation	.40
Wilks Lamda	.84

Table 5-7.   Classification of Respondents into Subgroups

	Predicted Group Membership*	
	1	2
Group 1:		
Board of Catholic Social Services	43%	57%
Group 2:		
Board of Catholic Education	27%	73%

*59% of all cases correctly classified.

The results of this analysis seem to indicate that board member characteristics are tied to funding needs. The inability to accurately predict group membership based on these characteristics indicates a need for more refinement in the development of variables used to measure member characteristics. Such refinement should be designed to enable much better identification of important resource suppliers and of the nature of linkages developed between them and the religious organization.

Discussion

While the initial predictions that advisory boards could serve to link the diocese, as a unit, to external groups did not receive much support, the data do, nevertheless, suggest linking roles for each board. Intensive study of the Archdiocese of Indianapolis clearly shows that while formally following a very autocratic authority structure, a great deal of defacto decentralization has occurred.

The archbishop *is* the diocese and, formally, has final approval on all issues. In interviews it was, in fact, revealed that one organizational problem is that of needing to somewhat restrict the number of people and problems with which the archbishop must deal.

Because of this very autocratic and absolute authority structure no "board of directors" can possibly exist formally. Nevertheless, a great deal of decentralization in decision making is also allowed. Individual agencies, many with their own advisory boards (such as the two studied), enjoy a great deal of authority within the frameworks of Catholic doctrine and diocesan policy. While the archbishop can and does occasionally intervene in decisions, these smaller units are largely left to run themselves and, apparently, are frequently responsible for providing a significant amount of their own program support. This is especially clear from the study of Catholic Social Services. This decision making and support independence has developed into a very loose "federated" structure. The smaller units then act, to a great extent, as independent organizations. Because they must obtain their own "supplies" (funding) they have adopted their own arrangements to reduce uncertainties in supply. These arrangements would be predicted by resource dependence theory and appear to be reflected in the findings of the present study of the Archdiocese of Indianapolis.

Predictions that board membership would *not* be based primarily on functional expertise and that board size would *not* be based on task size were largely supported by data from both boards. But in moving from these "negative" predictions to more "positive" predictions regarding attempts to link board membership to specific needs, statistical support became very weak if it existed at all. This is because the advisory boards provide linkages to very agency-specific constituencies rather than to constituencies which provide funding for the diocese as a whole. By focusing on both the needs and suppliers of the specific agencies the discriminant analysis uncovers differences which do appear to reflect efforts to use advisory boards to provide ties to important funding sources.

The findings of the study of the Archdiocese of Indianapolis do appear to indicate that resource dependence theory can be applied in the religious as well as the secular sphere. The more loosely coupled or "federated" structure in this case, however, suggests that advisory boards as linking devices have a much more limited value. Attempts to identify important constituencies at the diocesan level through use of a resource dependence framework will probably need to focus on devices other than advisory board memberships (although pastoral councils, once they have become established, may prove useful in such research).

Limitations of the Case Study

The findings of the study of the Archdiocese of Indianapolis are very limited. The two boards selected were chosen, in part, because they could be found in most U.S. dioceses. Nevertheless, this fact alone does not allow generalization of the findings to other dioceses of the Catholic church, much less to units of other religious organizations. In an effort to assess their potential for generalization to other dioceses of the Catholic church these findings were used to develop a survey which was sent to all 168 Catholic dioceses in the United States. While the results of this survey still do not allow generalization beyond the Catholic church in the United States, the findings do enable a more general discussion of authority, decentralization, and related management arrangements in the Catholic church. The findings of this survey and their possible implications are the subject of chapter 6. The predictions regarding the links between individual dioceses and the Vatican are also discussed there.

6

Generalizing: A National Survey of Diocesan Linkages

Purpose

As noted in chapter 5, if the Archdiocese of Indianapolis is, for some reason, a unique Catholic diocese, then it is possible that resource dependence theory could be applied more successfully to other dioceses. If we consider this research complete at this point, and rely only on the Indianapolis findings, it would be impossible to determine if the results were generalizable to other dioceses. For this reason a questionnaire was sent to other Roman Catholic dioceses nationwide. The primary purpose of this chapter is to discuss the findings of that questionnaire with particular emphasis on the generalizability of the findings of the case study. In many cases it will be possible to use the data from this structured questionnaire to provide more concise information on variables studied in the previous chapter and for applying this model to the Catholic church in general.

Research Methods

Resource dependence theory suggests that the munificence of the environment affects the linkage of the organization to its environment. Specifically, it is predicted that a more munificent environment will allow an organization to survive with fewer and looser links to its resource suppliers than would be the case for an organization facing a hostile environment. A 1975 study by Staw and Szwajkowski suggests that a relationship may exist between environmental scarcity and increased efforts to secure inputs.[1,2] This aspect of resource dependence theory may be used to attempt to generalize the results of the case study to the larger population of Catholic dioceses in the United States.

 Two measures of munificence are used in this research. One measure is developed by looking at the size of the Catholic population in the area of the diocese studied; specifically, the percentage of the entire population who are declared Catholics. If 80 percent of the people living within the physical area of a diocese are Catholic, it might be assumed that the environment is munificent. Because a large percentage of the population is Catholic, the diocese in such an area would not have a pressing need to develop the more planned linkages studied in chapter 5. It would enjoy a very large base of parishioners which would automatically give the diocese a strong presence in community affairs, in the minds of legislators from the area, and within the many other organizations in the community. If the environment locally is munificent in this sense one would also expect that relations with the Vatican could be less frequent because the diocese would have strong bases of support elsewhere and could, therefore, afford to be less attentive to links with Rome.

Within the physical boundaries of the Archdiocese of Indianapolis, on the other hand, Catholics represent only about 20 percent of the total population. In dioceses such as this a more planned and systematic effort by the diocesan hierarchy to develop linkages with important constituencies in its environment would be expected. Because Catholics make up only a small portion of the community, informal links with other organizations cannot be taken for granted but, rather, must be sought out more systematically. One might also expect a slightly closer relationship with Rome in cases where munificence in the local environment is low. A stronger linkage with the Vatican might help a diocese in this situation to gain legitimacy with its other constituencies because it would appear to be connected to, and to represent, the resources of a much more powerful organization.

The second measure of munificence used in this research is the percent of the diocese's operating income obtained from parishes in the diocese. If a very large portion of a diocese's funding is obtained directly from Catholics in the diocese it would be logical to expect that there would be less need for the diocese to link itself with other organizations for the purpose of securing sources of funding. If, on the other hand, Catholic parishioners supply a relatively smaller portion of a diocese's income, a much greater effort on the part of that diocese to link itself to additional funding would be expected.

The two measures just described represent two separate dimensions of munificence. The first could be labeled environmental connectivity. It is predicted that the more interconnected a diocese is with its broader environment (through its parishioners), the less concern it will need to show for forming other linkages. The second dimension of munificence might be labeled environmental support. It is expected that the nature and direction of support will determine the nature and direction of additional linkages sought by the diocese. Specifically, if a diocese enjoys a great deal of internal funding support it will not need to systematically seek many formal external linkages.

If, in studying other dioceses nationwide, these predictions are verified, it will indicate that the resource dependence model can be applied to the study of the Roman Catholic church using dioceses as the basic unit of analysis. It would also clearly show that the Archdiocese of Indianapolis is atypical. In the case study, contrary to the predictions just described, the Archdiocese was found to be loosely coupled to all three constituencies (local community, Vatican, and other organizations). Evidence of a systematic effort by the Archdiocese to link itself with the constituencies mentioned, an effort expected in a diocese in an environment which was not unusually munificent (in the case of Indianapolis, only 20 percent Catholic), was lacking in the case study. Indianapolis clearly does not fit the above predictions and it appears that this may be because boundary-spanning activities are centered elsewhere, specifically in the parishes and in the individual agencies of the diocese. If the findings of the national survey indicate the same loose coupling with constituencies that should be of importance to Catholic dioceses, it would then appear that Indianapolis is, in fact, typical of dioceses generally. A study of the relationship between munificence and variables measuring the degree of linkage of U.S. dioceses with important constituencies in their environments should, therefore, help to answer the question, stated at the end of chapter 5, as to how representative Indianapolis is of Catholic dioceses in the U.S. in general.

Before moving on it should also be noted that the two measures of munificence to be used were found to be unrelated ($r = -.0284$, $p = .404$). This is to be expected if they do, in fact, represent two separate dimensions of munificence, as suggested.

The Sample

A questionnaire was developed on the basis of information obtained during the study of the Archdiocese of Indianapolis (see app. J). Almost all questions were designed so that respondents answered using Likert-type scales rather than the more open format used for the questionnaires sent to board members in the case study. Items 1:77 and 1:78 were the questions used to measure munificence on the basis described above. This questionnaire was sent to the chancellors (or a similar centrally placed official if a chancellor was not available) of all 168 dioceses in the United States, including Alaska and Hawaii. Of the 168 questionnaires sent, 79 (47.0 percent) were returned in time to be included in the analysis. As with the questionnaires sent to board members, the unusually high response to this questionnaire by individuals facing many other demands on their time was very encouraging.

The results of the national survey are listed in appendix K. This appendix shows the frequencies with which respondents chose from the responses available on each question. In most cases responses are shown both for the entire set of respondents and also broken down on the basis of the proportion of Catholics in an area. The responses are broken down in this way to attempt to highlight possible differences between dioceses in areas of differing Catholic concentrations (one of the munificence measures mentioned above which appears as item 70 in app. K).

Results

Board Composition

Several of the questionnaire items seek information regarding characteristics of diocesan board members, specifically with respect to the boards of education and social services, both of which are found to exist in the vast majority of cases. The first variable to be correlated with the munificence measures was the percent of each board representing lay people (or outside membership). For simplicity in this discussion, and in the tables, the two munificence variables will be referred to as connectivity and support (see table 6-1).

Table 6-1.   Percent of Boards Representing Lay People

Percent of Boards Representing Lay People with Percent of Catholics in Area (Connectivity)	
Education: −.0355	Social Services: −.0421
p = .379	p = .359

Percent of Boards Representing Lay People with Support of Catholics (Support)	
Education: .0291	Social Services: .2628
p = .401	p = .011

If the predictions are accurate it is expected that, as munificence goes up, outside membership, or the percent of lay people on the board, should drop. This negative relationship is predicted because if environmental support and connectivity are already high there is little need for increases in outside membership for the purpose of creating links with the external environment. Because of the way in which the responses to these questions are listed (see app. K, items 84 and 94) these expected results should show up in table 6-1 as positive correlations for both munificence measures. In three of the four cases no significant relationship is found between either of the munificence measures and outside board membership. A significant relationship ($p < .05$) in the predicted direction does, however, appear between support and social services outside membership, providing only very limited support for the predictions.

Several questions are also asked of respondents as to the characteristics which they feel are important in people serving on diocesan boards. The responses to these questions are correlated with the munificence variables for the boards of education and social services in table 6-2. Several dioceses also have a pastoral council (which does not currently exist in the Archdiocese of Indianapolis). Several questions regarding desired personnel characteristics of pastoral council members are, therefore, also asked, the results of which are correlated with the munificence variables in table 6-3.

Table 6-2. Correlations of Munificence Measures with Member Characteristics for the Boards of Education and Social Services

Item Code	With Connectivity		With Support	
	Education	Social Services	Education	Social Services
85/95	.0425 p = .369	-.0629 p = .304	-.1004 p = .219	.1852 p = .067
86/96	.0796 p = .266	.1162 p = .171	.1345 p = .149	.0390 p = .377
87/97	.0852 p = .252	.0908 p = .299	.1580 p = .110	.1281 p = .151
88/98	.1788 p = .080	.1462 p = .115	.0719 p = .291	-.1653 p = .091
89/99	.0683 p = .296	-.0454 p = .359	-.0466 p = .360	-.1210 p = .171
90/100	-.1905 p = .066	-.1184 p = .168	.1367 p = .145	.1587 p = .101

Key to Item Codes (item numbers match those in app. K):

85/95 Active in parish organizations
86/96 Active in non-church community organizations
87/97 Have experience in other diocesan-wide committees and activities
88/98 Are affiliated with other educators/social service organizations in the community
89/99 Are affiliated with important groups in the community
99/100 Have knowledge and/or experience in the field

If the predictions are correct it is expected that, in table 6-2, the munificence measures will be negatively correlated with the measures of the importance of outside attachments (86/96, 88/98, 89/99). In other words, if support and connectivity are high then the need for members to act as linking devices is low, which should be expressed in terms of a weak desire for these characteristics in board members. In all instances, however, the correlations are both low and insignificant. The predictions here are clearly not realized with respect to the boards of education or social services as expressed by the absence of any relationship in this case.

The opposite relationship might be predicted between the munificence variables and the questions regarding internal activity (85/95, 87/97). That is, where internal support is high, or where Catholics make up a large portion of the population, it might be expected that participation in parish or diocesan activities would be seen as a more important prerequisite for board membership. Positive correlations between these variables are, therefore, expected. Looking at table 6-2, low and insignificant correlations are again found. The predictions appear, therefore, to be unsupportable on the basis of the relation of board of education or board of social services characteristics to munificence.

Table 6-3.   Correlations of Munificence Measures with Member Characteristics for the Pastoral Council

Item Code	With Connectivity	With Support
56	.0911 p = .215	.1154 p = .162
57	.1239 p = .143	.0175 p = .441
58	0 p = .500	−.0175 p = .441
59	.2237 p = .026	−.0114 p = .462
60	.0594 p = .313	.1197 p = .165

Key to Item Codes (item numbers match those in app. K):

56   Active in parish organizations
57   Active in non-church community organizations
58   Have a knowledge of the organization
       of the diocese
59   Have experience in other diocesan-wide
       committees and activities
60   Be able to represent specific groups
       and/or current concerns of the community

Looking at characteristics of pastoral council members in table 6-3, we are also unable to find support for the predictions. All of the correlations here are low and all but one are insignificant. The one significant correlation occurs between connectivity and item 59. The direction of the correlation would seem to indicate that where connectivity is high, experience in other diocesan activities is important. This may be interpreted to mean that, when a large portion of an area's population is Catholic, aspirants for the pastoral council must distinguish themselves in diocesan service to be considered for a post on the council. If this interpretation is correct these results would provide some weak support for the predictions. If a large portion of the community is Catholic it might be logical to expect that internal activity could be given priority because external links would, in many cases, already be provided.

Conclusions on Board Composition

From the results just discussed it is clear that support for the application of resource dependence theory, based on study of the relationship of board composition to munificence, is lacking. In all but two cases the relationships found are insignificant and two significant correlations cannot, by any stretch of the imagination, be considered strong support. It appears, therefore, that board composition is not significantly affected by the munificence of the environment. This seems to indicate that diocesan boards do not act primarily as linking devices to groups in a diocese's environment. These findings tend to support those of the case study of the Archdiocese of Indianapolis. However, it will be recalled that in that case the diocese appeared to be a federation of relatively loosely joined parishes and agencies. There was evidence that resource dependence theory might best be applied to the individual boards and their individual sources of support. In the context of the case study it did appear that board composition was, to a certain extent, related to sources of board funding rather than to diocesan-wide support. Before moving beyond the study of board composition this possibility will be assessed using the national data.

Board Differences

Table 6-4 shows the relationship between the size of outside membership and the sources of funding for each type of board. For education boards insignificant relationships are found. In this situation, however, this is what might be expected. Only internal sources of funding for boards of education are studied and no relationship between internal funding sources and the size of outside memberships on these boards would be predicted.

Table 6-4.   Percent of Board Representing Lay People with Board
Funding Sources

Education		Social Services	
Tuition:	.0096	Parishes:	.2360
	p = .470		p = .024
Parishes:	.0061	Diocese:	.3546
	p = .480		p = .001
Diocese:	-.0819	United Way &	
	p = .257	Similar Sources:	-.2080
			p = .041
		Fees Charged:	-.0498
			p = .340
		Government:	-.1267
			p = .150
		Businesses:	.0256
			p = .417

For boards of social services, on the other hand, three of six correlations computed are significant ($p < .05$). The relationships here are also, in all cases, in the direction that would have been expected (again, because of the wording of questions regarding size of outside membership, a negative correlation in this case represents a positive relationship). The three correlations appear to show that outside membership tends to be lower in situations where parishes or the diocese provide large amounts of board funding. On the other hand, outside membership (which, it will be recalled, is interpreted as lay membership) tends to be higher in cases in which agencies such as the United Way provide significant amounts of funding. While the correlations are not particularly high, they are clearly in the directions expected.

Tables 6-5 and 6-6 show the relationships between board funding sources and desired board member characteristics for the boards of education and social services respectively. It is expected that the items which emphasize outward-looking characteristics (specifically items 86, 88, and 89 for education and 96, 98, and 99 for social services) should be positively correlated with external sources of funding. As these are characteristics of individuals who are active in the community and would, therefore, provide linkages with external sources of funding, these characteristics would be more in demand on boards which rely more heavily on external funding. Conversely, the items which emphasize inward-looking characteristics (specifically items 85 and 87 for education and 95 and 97 for social services) should be positively correlated with internal suppliers of funds, possibly at the expense of external linkages.

Table 6-5.   Correlations of Sources of Funding with Desired Member Characteristics for Boards of Education

Item Code	From Tuition	From Parishes	Allocation by Diocese
85	.0170 p = .448	-.1976 p = .060	-.0447 p = .364
86	-.0369 p = .388	.2285 p = .036	-.0079 p = .475
87	.0913 p = .240	-.1081 p = .200	.1086 p = .199
88	.1208 p = .177	.1691 p = .094	-.0963 p = .228
89	-.0190 p = .442	-.0275 p = .415	.0992 p = .220
90	.0639 p = .311	.0827 p = .260	-.1328 p = .150

Key to Item Codes (item numbers match those in app. K):

85   Active in parish organizations
86   Active in non-church community organizations
87   Have experience in other diocesan-wide
      committees and activities
88   Are affiliated with other educators
      in the community
89   Are affiliated with important groups
      in the community
90   Have knowledge and/or experience in
      the field of education

In looking at table 6-5, positive relationships between the three sources of funding listed (all of which are internal in the case of boards of education) and the two variables (85 and 87) which look at desired levels of church-related activity are expected. Unfortunately, none of the correlations are significant. The one correlation that is significant for boards of education is between item number 86 and the level of funding received from parishes. This relationship seems to indicate that where parish funding is a large part of the board of education's (or school system's) revenues it is important to find people who are active in the community to serve on the board. It is possible that people who are generally active are felt, in this case, to provide good links to the parishes as well; however, these results are difficult to account for.

Table 6-6.   Correlations of Sources of Funding with Desired Member
Characteristics for Boards of Social Services

Item Code	Parishes	Diocese	United Way	Fees Charged	Government	Business
95	.1896	.1260	−.1321	−.2104	−.1141	.1314
	p = .059	p = .153	p = .140	p = .041	p = .179	p = .145
96	−.0829	.0301	−.0964	−.0053	.1124	.0746
	p = .249	p = .404	p = .215	p = .483	p = .183	p = .274
97	.0636	−.0022	−.0243	−.0783	.1526	.2439
	p = .302	p = .493	p = .422	p = .261	p = .109	p = .023
98	−.1849	.0585	.0763	.1579	.1274	−.2889
	p = .064	p = .318	p = .267	p = .097	p = .152	p = .009
99	−.2905	−.0649	.0177	.0981	.2805	.0446
	p = .009	p = .304	p = .444	p = .217	p = .012	p = .363
100	−.2380	.0803	.0533	−.0032	.1786	.1247
	p = .025	p = .259	p = .333	p = .490	p = .074	p = .159

Key to Item Codes (item numbers match those in app. K):

95   Active in parish organizations
96   Active in non-church community organizations
97   Have experience in other diocesan-wide
      committees and activities
98   Are affiliated with other social serivce
      organizations in the community
99   Are affiliated with important groups
      in the community
100 Have knowledge and/or experience in
      the field of social work

Table 6-6 shows the relationships between boards of social services' sources of funding and desired member characteristics. In this case six of the relationships do appear to be significant. The relationship between item 95 (activity in parish organizations) and income derived from fees charged to clients is in the direction expected. If a large portion of income is derived from clients, internal links to churches in the diocese would become less important. The relationships between item 99 and both income from parishes and funding from governments are also in the predicted directions. If a large part of the budget is supplied by government grants, affiliation with other community groups (which probably include government agencies and officials) should be important, as is suggested by the positive correlation. On the other hand, where parish funding is important, affiliation with other community groups should be less important. This expectation also seems to hold given the negative correlation between parish-sourced income and item 99. The relationship between funding supplied by business organizations and items 97 and 98 are, however, the exact opposite of expectations. Experience in other diocesan activities seems to be important here as expressed in the positive correlation between this item and funding supplied by businesses. This may, however, be understandable if individuals who are active in the diocese also have a high profile in the community and, in the course of their service, do build up links to other community organizations, including local businesses. The relationship between affiliations with other social service organizations (item 98) and business funding is negative. While initially predicting that outside linkages and outside funding would be positively related, the negative relationship in this case may make some sense. If businesses provide much funding then links with social service organizations might be downplayed in favor of other links which may be more important. Links with social service agencies might also indicate greater professionalism in the area supervised. Affiliation with social service groups may indicate a professional interest in social services. If this is true, and if people are selected to the board partially on the basis of their ability to form links with important resource suppliers, then this relationship would make sense where businesses are important fund suppliers. The negative relationship may, indirectly, suggest that fewer professionals in the field (people who would be active in social services organizations) would be chosen in favor of other individuals who could provide more direct links to important resource suppliers.

No attempt was made to predict the relationship between item 100, knowledge or experience in the field of social work, and the sources of funds. If, as was predicted in the original research hypotheses, expertise in the function supervised is unrelated to selection to the board, then negative relationships between this item and all possible sources of funds might be predicted. If board members are chosen primarily for their ability to link the organization to funding sources then expertise would be less important where a given source of funding is critical. The ability to select a board of experts in the area supervised would be sacrificed in order to build a set of linkages. The significant negative correlation between item 100 and parish funding does, therefore, appear to be understandable within the context of earlier expectations.

Looking at figure 6-1, it also appears that an interesting parallel can be drawn between the findings of the case study and the findings of the national survey. It can be seen that on questions which assessed activity in internal or church organizations (85/95, 87/97), members of the board of education scored higher. On the other hand, on questions 86/96, 88/98, and 89/99, which assessed outside community activity, members of the board of social

Figure 6-1. Comparison of Board Member Characteristics from National Questionnaire

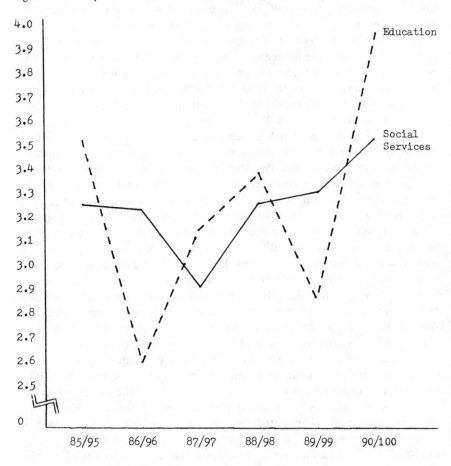

85/95   Active in parish organizations
86/96   Active in non-church community organizations
87/97   Have experience in other diocesan-wide committees and activities
88/98   Are affiliated with other educators/social services organizations
        in the community
89/99   Are affiliated with important groups in the community
90/100 Have knowledge and/or experience in the field

services ranked higher. The only exception is question 88/98, which asks about affiliation with others of the same profession. However, looking at the t-statistics in table 6-7 it is seen that the difference between the responses for the two boards is insignificant at the $p < .05$ level on question 88/98 on which the expected results were reversed. In all other cases the differences in the responses with respect to each group are significant and parallel differences found in the case study.

Table 6-7.   t-Statistics for Questions Comparing Board Member
Characteristics

Question 85 with Question 95	t-value = 2.96 DF = 59 P = .004
Question 86 with Question 96	t-value = -4.19 DF = 59 P = .000
Question 87 with Question 97	t-value = 2.95 DF = 59 P = .005
Question 88 with Question 98	t-value = 1.49 DF = 58 P = .140
Question 89 with Question 99	t-value = -2.59 DF = 56 P = .012
Question 90 with Question 100	t-value = 4.07 DF = 58 P = .000

Conclusions on Board Differences

While in several cases the relationships studied were nonsignificant (at the $p <$ .05 level) there does appear to be a fair amount of evidence that the composition of diocesan boards nationwide, as in Indianapolis, is in part based on sources of board funding. In most cases where significant relationships were found the correlations were in the direction predicted. Considering these findings together with those of the study of relationships between munificence and board composition it appears, at this point, that the findings of the case study are reflected in the study of other dioceses. The almost complete absence of significant relationships between munificence and board composition suggests that little formal effort at this diocesan level is made to develop links to the community. This would indicate, as was found in the case study, that dioceses are loosely coupled to the local community. The somewhat stronger findings with respect to board differences suggest that, as in the Archdiocese of Indianapolis, individual agencies and parishes are only loosely connected with the structure of the diocese. Board composition is more closely related to the needs of the individual board (or agency) than to the needs of the diocese as a whole.

Relationships to the Rest of the Catholic Church

It was earlier hypothesized that, because Rome supplies few important resources, a diocese will tend to neglect ties with the Vatican in favor of more important resource suppliers. If, however, the local environment is not munificent, it might be expected that ties with Rome would become somewhat stronger. A diocese which is located, for example, in an area of low Catholic population (low connectivity) might seek more legitimacy or a higher profile by more closely identifying itself with the larger church worldwide. In these circumstances the diocese should also seek more contact with other units of the church such as other dioceses, the Apostolic Delegate, or the National Conference of Catholic Bishops.

Table 6-8 shows three significant relationships when comparing the munificence scores with variables assessing the amount of contact dioceses have with other parts of the Roman Catholic church. Of these, however, only one is in the direction predicted. This is the relationship of support to the frequency of consultation with other church units. As might be expected, when parishioner giving is low, contact and consultation with other Catholic dioceses increases. This relationship is clear in the strong negative correlation of these two variables ($r = -.3079$, $p < .05$). It makes sense because it is possible that other dioceses might be able to provide support to the struggling diocese (e.g., interviews did indicate that, on a very limited basis, low interest loans can be made by one diocese to another).

The relationships between connectivity and frequency of travel to Rome and between connectivity and frequency of meetings with other bishops in the province are, however, the reverse of those expected (because of the wording of these questions, and the question on travel to Washington, a negative correlation indicates that when connectivity is high within a diocese, frequency of travel or contact is also high). Both of these correlations are significant ($p < .05$) but show that, as the portion of the total population which is Catholic increases, travel to Rome and frequency of provincial meetings also goes up. A possible explanation for this unexpected result may be found by considering the nature of dioceses which enjoy predominantly Catholic populations. Looking at large dioceses such as the Archdioceses of

Table 6-8.   Diocesan Contact with Other Units of the Catholic Church

	Connectivity	Support
Frequency of Travel to Rome by Bishop	-.2151 p = .031	-.0887 p = .225
Frequency of Travel to Washington, DC by Bishop	-.0015 p = .495	.0624 p = .306
Frequency of Consultation with Rome or Washington, DC	.0538 p = .320	-.1430 p = .107
Frequency of Consultation with Other Church Units (Dioceses)	-.0564 p = .312	-.3079 p = .003
Activity in National Bishops' Organizations	-.0477 p = .339	-.0472 p = .342
Frequency of Meetings with Other Bishops in Province	-.2478 p = .015	-.0270 p = .408

Chicago, New York, or Boston, it is noteworthy that these are dioceses which have regularly been outspoken in the church and whose prelates have been, at least recently, very active among the U.S. Catholic bishops. It seems possible, therefore, that dioceses which have large Catholic populations are, by their nature, more active as "leaders" in the U.S. Catholic church. If this is so, increased travel and activity on the part of the ordinary of such a diocese might be expected in his role as a more national leader, explaining the unexpected results in table 6-8.

Conclusions on Relationships to the Rest of the Catholic Church

As was the case with board composition, there is some suggestion that the munificence of the environment affects the relationship of the diocese to other units of the church (specifically Rome, the apostolic delegate, and other dioceses). The evidence, however, is very weak, which would seem to once again suggest very loose coupling between the local community and the diocese on the one hand, and the diocese and the Vatican on the other. If the proposed explanation of the unexpected relationship between connectivity and travel to Rome is correct, it could conceivably provide further support for the proposition that Rome provides few resources and, therefore, that links with Rome and a diocese may be increased because a particular diocese is an important leader in the national church and, therefore important to Rome. It would appear, however, that increased contact with Rome does not result from needs of a diocese to replace support by one constituency with increased linkage to another.

Relationships to Other Organizations

Resource dependence theory suggests that the diocese's relationship to other organizations will also be affected by the munificence of the environment. In this case it might be predicted that as support is reduced connections with other organizations will be increased. Unfortunately, table 6-9 shows all of the correlations with support are below the desired significance level ($p < .05$), all but one being essentially zero order correlations. It is interesting to note that the relationship between support and joint activity with other faiths is in the predicted direction. When support for the Catholic church in a community is low, one way of increasing its influence is to join forces with other major faiths in the community. As noted, however, the correlation in this case is not significant.

Table 6-9.   Diocesan Contact with Non-Catholic Organizations

| | Munificence | |
	Connectivity	Support
With Government Agencies	.1579	.0073
	p = .084	p = .475
With Businesses	.2659	.0575
	p = .009	p = .310
With Other Major Faiths	–.0160	–.1272
	p = .178	p = .135
Diocese Formal Member of Community-	.0448	.0448
Wide Ecumenical Organization	p = .350	p = .350
Clergy Activity in Local Ministerial	.0373	–.0613
Organizations	p = .373	p = .298
Ordinary Activity in	.1082	.0439
Local Community	p = .173	p = .352
Ordinary Travel to	–.1638	.0264
Parishes in Diocese	p = .076	p = .410

It is more difficult to predict the relationship between munificence measured in terms of the proportion of Catholics in an area (connectivity) and efforts at linking the diocese to other organizations. To a certain extent it might be expected that if Catholics make up a large portion of the population the diocese will not face a great need to seek out other links. "Saturation" of the community by its parishioners would automatically provide the diocese with several links to important organizations. On the other hand, it is also possible that, in a largely Catholic community, major organizations may find themselves drawn into closer cooperation with and support of church programs. This may be the case in the one significant relationship in table 6-9. Apparently in communities with large Catholic populations there is a greater tendency for joint activities with business organizations. Other correlations, while not significant, appear to be in a logical direction. Where Catholic population is low, such as in the Archdiocese of Indianapolis, the ordinary might be expected to attempt to foster diocesan unity by a great deal of travel to individual parishes. While not significant at a $p < .05$ level, the correlation between ordinary travel to parishes and connectivity appears to suggest that this might be the case in other Catholic dioceses as well as in Indianapolis.

Conclusions on Relationships to Other Organizations

With only one significant correlation in table 6-9 it is not possible to conclude that a relationship exists between munificence and linkages to other organizations. While there are a few interesting correlations, these results would seem once again to indicate, at best, a very loose coupling by Catholic dioceses to other organizations.

General Discussion of Survey Results

It is quite clear from the above analysis that a consistent relationship between munificence and variables designed to measure efforts by dioceses to link themselves with their constituencies has not been found. Predominant in all of the statistics generated is the veritable absence of significant relationships. Frequently, when a significant relationship is found it is in the opposite direction from that predicted using resource dependence theory. No relationship between munificence and board composition is found with the data from the national survey. It is possible that linkages to Rome may have more to do with the importance of the diocese as a leader in its region than with Rome's importance to the diocese. A relationship between munificence and efforts by dioceses to link themselves to other organizations in the environment is also not found. The virtual absence of significant correlations between munificence and variables assessing linkages suggests that, as was the case in the Archdiocese of Indianapolis, Catholic dioceses tend to be loosely coupled to the constituencies studied in this research. There is no evidence that boundary-spanning activity occurs predominantly at the diocesan level.

The fact that data from the national survey did show some significant differences between the boards of education and social services also suggests that Indianapolis is typical of most U.S. dioceses with respect to the actual location of most boundary-spanning activity. Evidence does suggest, particularly in the case of boards of social services, that characteristics of board members do vary to some extent with the sources of board funding.

Relationships between desired board member characteristics (see fig. 6-1) do parallel board member characteristics which surfaced in the Indianapolis study. This suggests that, as was found in Indianapolis, boundary spanning in a Roman Catholic diocese may be more likely to occur at the level of individual agencies and parishes rather than at the level of the diocesan hierarchy.

It would appear, therefore, that the failure to find strong support for resource dependence theory in the attempt to apply it to the Archdiocese of Indianapolis was not the result of poor selection of the diocese for study. Nothing in the national findings suggests that Indianapolis is in any way an atypical Roman Catholic diocese (at least within the United States). The most logical conclusion appears, therefore, to be the conclusion first suggested in chapter 5. It seems likely that, due to the relatively loose structure of a diocese, efforts to create links to suppliers of important resources are probably centered at a lower level within the diocesan unit. Specifically, boundary spanning appears to be centered at the level of individual parishes and agencies within a diocese.

7

An Adaptive, Decentralized Bureaucracy

Review of the Study

The purpose of this research is twofold. First, an effort is made to highlight the importance of religious organizations as actors in the economic and political environments. Second, one particular religious organization, the Roman Catholic church, is closely studied in an attempt to introduce a management model to the study of religious groups focusing on their organizational qualities.

The resource dependence model, with its primarily external (to the organization under study) focus, allows the integration of both these objectives throughout this study. In the early chapters emphasis is placed on the potential relationships between the religious and secular environments. The latter half of the book seeks to use a resource dependence framework to explore possible channels of influence between religious and secular groups. In taking this approach much information regarding the management of the focal organization, the Catholic church, is highlighted. This knowledge, as will be seen shortly, may be useful for managing other organizations as well.

A unique benefit of the approach used in this research comes from the fact that it involves a nested design which includes study of the church at three different organizational levels: the overall organization, the diocese, and diocesan subunits. In essence chapter 2 provides a case study of the worldwide church organization over time as it relates to the economic and political environments. In chapters 5 and 6 two different approaches are used to study diocesan units of the Catholic church. While the analysis in these two chapters focuses primarily on the diocesan unit of organization it was also necessary, however, to collect considerable information on subunits of the dioceses. As a result much was also learned about the organizations of various Catholic agencies and service units and, to a very limited extent, about parish structure. This nested design allows assessment of the application of the resource dependence model over a broad range of organizational levels. The result is an enhanced ability to assess the applicability of resource dependence theory to religious organizations and to suggest approaches for more effective future study. As this study is primarily exploratory, this in itself is a worthwhile result.

Another benefit of the research design used is that it involved two different methods of analysis. Rather than rely solely on longitudinal case studies, a comparative study of a cross-section of organizational units (dioceses) was also included to help provide more concise and insightful information on the Catholic organization.

In any research, problems are discovered and shortcomings recognized during or near the completion of study which the researcher was unable to predict in the beginning. This research is not an exception. While many minor problems were encountered, three major areas can be cited which severely reduce the value of the findings.

First of all, it was found that a Roman Catholic diocese is a much looser federation of parishes and agencies than was originally expected. While this added to the research in the form of striking contrasts between the individual boards studied, it also made it impossible to identify boundary-spanning units which might function to link the diocese, *as a single unit*, to important groups in its environment. No unit could be found which functions to link a diocese to its environment in a manner similar to that found in research on business organizations.

A second problem was discovered in data collection. While everyone contacted in the Archdiocese of Indianapolis was extremely helpful, many going well out of their way to provide information, there were still many gaps in the available data. As happens frequently in longitudinal studies that rely on historical data, data for earlier years were often incomplete. As a result, analysis often had to be based on a period of ten years or less. As was evident in the correlations used to study board characteristics in chapter 5, this often meant the significance of statistics cited was low. This was overcome, to some extent, by concentrating on trends or shifts in the data. However, the findings would have been much more conclusive had more years of data been available.

Finally, a problem was encountered in contacting the diocesan prelates to determine what problems were faced by the diocese. Many of the problems described involved either internal church issues, such as clergy shortages, or moral issues, such as teen drinking and drug abuse. While it cannot be denied that these are serious problems, it is difficult, if not impossible given the ambiguous nature of these issues, to use them in the resource dependence framework. It would appear that these concerns could fit the model but involve resources which are beyond the diocese's control. Also, as these were seen as Catholic concerns, those interviewed envisioned no possibilities of cooperation with other community organizations for the purpose of dealing with them. If external community concerns had surfaced more often than they did it might have been feasible to match them more effectively with the activities of church boundary spanners.

The type of problems that surfaced in the interviews are understandable given the position in the hierarchy of many of those interviewed. While the prelates interviewed also frequently serve as parish priests, their offices necessitate that many focus primary attention on diocesan administrative and spiritual problems. It is understandable that such problems would be on the minds of these individuals when they were interviewed. Among the few who were not serving in administrative roles in the diocesan hierarchy other issues surfaced as important. Therefore, there is reason to believe that had others been interviewed, such as "full-time" parish priests and other lay functionaries, a larger number of community issues and resource-sharing concerns might have been identified.

Discussion of the Findings

The results of this attempt to use resource dependence theory in the study of the Catholic church appear at first to be somewhat confusing and contradictory. In chapter 2 it seems clear that the church overall is enmeshed in and somewhat responsive to its environment. We see an organization structure closely related to that of the Roman Empire. Christian writings very clearly support positions which would be beneficial to church interests and appear to react predictably to threats to a stable society. More recently it appears that the Second Vatican Council may be seen, at least partially, as an effort by the church worldwide to become more responsive to important constituencies in its environment.

The diocesan studies, however, reveal an apparently different situation. In chapters 5 and 6 attempts to apply resource dependence theory to diocesan units appear to be generally unsuccessful. In these studies dioceses are found to be, at best, only loosely coupled to the different constituencies with which they must interact.

On the other hand, at the lowest level of aggregation studied some evidence to support the model is found. While study did not focus initially on diocesan subunits, there is some significant evidence suggesting that the resource dependence model can be most effectively applied at this level. While not predicting differences between the board of education and the board of social services, differences are uncovered which are predominantly in the directions that would have been predicted using resource dependence theory. This appears to be true of both the case study and the national survey results. Evidence is also uncovered, in the case study of the Archdiocese of

Indianapolis, which indicates that boundary-spanning activities might be concentrated predominantly at the parish level. This finding is in line with research done by Richard Guerrette, who suggests that priests are important boundary-spanning individuals in the Catholic church (see chap. 4).

To properly interpret these results we need to consider some of the more unique aspects of the Catholic church as an organization and of its environment. First of all, it would seem that, in general, the environment of the Catholic church today is relatively munificent. While there are certainly exceptions to this (the Soviet Union and some of its satellite countries come immediately to mind), clearly the environments of the dioceses studied in this research are munificent. In a munificent environment, as noted in chapter 6, an organization can afford to rely on relatively loose links to resource suppliers. There is also some evidence in chapters 5 and 6 that interdependence is spread across a large number of organizations locally and regionally which supply funding, priests, and parishioners. With dependence spread across many organizations (e.g., Rome; the United Way; federal, state, and local governments; community groups; men and women religious), links to any single group can be sparse and relatively loose. As a result, the effects of these groups on diocesan structure may be relatively small. Additionally, in some cases the demands of different groups on the diocese are probably in conflict and, as a result, their net impacts on structure may be even less noticeable.

On the other hand Catholic units at a lower level in the organization will, in most cases, have fewer suppliers of resources. Individual suppliers will control greater portions of critical resources (for example, consider the fact that in Indianapolis the United Way supplies 49 percent of the funding for Catholic Social Services). These units must compete not only with other community organizations for resources but with other Catholic agencies and parishes as well. At this level it is clear that developing links with other groups in the environment becomes much more important. Conversely, these groups are likely to have a much greater impact on the structure of the diocesan subunits than they do on the diocese as a whole. Parishes, which are primary suppliers of funding to the diocese, are relatively independent units within the loose federation of a diocese. As a result, they, too, are likely to be affected to some degree by demands from their own more localized suppliers.

The Vatican appears to be considerably more responsive to environmental pressures, is in a very different position from units at these other two levels of the Catholic organization. Throughout most of the church's history the Vatican has been forced to balance the strong and often conflicting demands of many actors in a frequently hostile environment (moderate success early in its history in dealing with such demands may, in part, explain why Rome is the preeminent see in the Catholic church although its location in Rome, the one-time capital of the empire, and another external consideration, undoubtedly had much to do with it). We can speculate, on the basis of resource dependence theory, as to the considerations behind some of the early mutations of the church discussed in chapter 2. For example, at the time the church's structure was developed it was a relatively weak institution dependent on the Roman Empire for societal legitimacy. The result was a structure closely modeled on the structure of the empire. With the fall of the empire the church stepped in to fill a vacuum. The church arrived at the apex of its power at a time when the only other governmental units were feudal states which were constantly at war, making the church the only source of stability in society. As the nation-state developed, however, the church found itself unable to successfully balance conflicting demands placed on it. Armies were now stronger and had to be feared by the pope (consider, for example, the position of Pope Clement VII when Henry VIII demanded annulment of his marriage to Catherine of Aragon, aunt of the Holy Roman Emperor Charles V). From this point and throughout the Reformation the church saw its power eroded as nation states came to dominate events in the Western world. Only recently, with improved communication and greater emphasis placed on the value of world forums, does the church seem to be enjoying some renewal of its past strength.

While much of this is speculation and does not prove the existence of causal relationships, it does seem to suggest reasons for the apparent contrast between the historical evidence regarding the international organization as opposed to the findings of the diocesan studies. It appears that the Diocese of Rome has historically been placed in a position which has forced it to be more concerned with external constituencies. While the pope is, importantly, a bishop, his focus has to be worldwide rather than local. He is forced to deal with governments and armies. Political events affecting any part of the church are, technically, his concern. While balancing conflicting and often threatening groups, he also needs to keep the church somewhat distant from these groups as well if the church is to have reasonable freedom of action (the captivity of the papacy at Avignon in France in the fourteenth century is a case in which the Vatican was unable to maintain its distance from important constituencies and which helped provide impetus for the Reformation).

The positions of units at three different levels of this very loosely structured organization may therefore explain the differing results obtained in this attempt to apply resource dependence theory. Clearly, at the three different levels demands on the organization differ considerably. Rome faces an environment that is not as munificent as that faced by the dioceses studied. The result is an organization which is at least moderately concerned with balancing environmental demands and, when necessary, creating linkages with important groups (although because links also restrict an organization's freedom to exert influence the church will also try to limit such linkages as much as possible).

At both the diocesan and subdiocesan levels in the sample studied the environment is much more munificent than is the environment faced now or in the past by the Vatican. Diocesan agencies, however, appear to be reliant on a much more limited set of resource suppliers. Individual suppliers control larger portions of necessary resources such as funding. As a result, at this lowest level of the Catholic organization, some clear evidence of important linking activity is found. The dioceses studied, however, would all be expected to face relatively munificent environments. It appears that they often have a large and diverse base of resource suppliers. Dioceses are, therefore, able to limit their linking activity to a greater extent than can either the Vatican or the diocesan subunits. It would seem that for this reason the dioceses studied show little structural variation which can be associated with environmental demands placed on them.

Therefore, the overall conclusion of this research is that resource dependence theory can be applied usefully to the Roman Catholic church. Unfortunately, while the organizational unit chosen for closest analysis did not yield the relationships originally predicted, other levels studied, albeit less intensively, do yield interesting results. If the above explanations are accurate it would appear that the Catholic church has been shaped to a considerable degree by its environment, as suggested by contingency theory as well as by resource dependence theory. The impact of the environment has, however, been different at different levels of this organization. The Catholic church also seems to provide a very good example of an organization which has adapted to considerable changes in its environment over time. In this sense its survival also becomes understandable in the context of the population ecology model which states that some organizational forms are selected (for survival) over others due to their better fit with environmental requirements. While the church is often condemned as being slow to change (or even unchanging), it can be seen in chapter 2 that the Catholic church has frequently amended its position and negotiating stance when environmental changes required it. The second Vatican Council seems to be, at least partially, its most recent attempt to do this, but evidence of this also exists in its apparent recent emphasis on using economic rather than political channels in attempting to exert influence (as noted in chap. 2).

Overall, these findings describe a very large and very formalized organization which is administered in a very decentralized manner. While the pope and the hierarchy of bishops and cardinals are very important in determining overall policy (doctrine and dogma), individual units, whether dioceses or intradiocesan agencies (or even extradiocesan groups such as religious orders), are left much to themselves in day-to-day functioning. There is evidence that these units influence, and are influenced by, numerous actors in their immediate environments. In some cases local change may eventually become so widespread as to have an impact on larger units of the church and even be reflected in canon law (this is what seems to be happening in the expansion of such things as business offices, priests' senates, and pastoral councils). In this way this very large, bureaucratic organization gives the impression of unchanging stability while constantly making administrative adjustments to local pressures. How quickly and efficiently this change takes place is another research question but it is clear that some considerable adjustment is bottom up (as opposed to Weber's description of pure bureaucracy). These mechanisms have apparently been adequate enough to ensure continued organizational survival and even, in recent times, an improving image and growing international role.

Limitations of the Study

The primary limitations of this study may be found in the fact that it is, essentially, exploratory. Answers to the research questions are generally very tentative. Some of the most useful findings of this book pertain to what can not be done using a diocese as a unit of study. Confirmation of expectations that resource dependence theory would be useful for studying religious groups organizationally is, at best, in need of further support. Information regarding other levels of the Catholic organization, while apparently fitting in logically with the diocesan findings and with other studies, primarily represents the outcomes of unplanned extensions of the initial investigation.

The most rigorous attempt to apply resource dependence theory to the study of religious organizations focused on only one unit of the Roman Catholic church: the Archdiocese of Indianapolis. This study, along with the historical information provided in chapter 2 and the findings of the nationwide survey reported in chapter 6, represents only the very beginnings of the organizational study of this large and complex bureaucracy. Additionally, while it is true that the national survey and church documents suggest that many of the diocesan structures studied should exist in most locations, the survey also suggests the possibility of some significant differences. The demands of different environments may result in very different structures in some regions. Units which appear to be replicated in several different regions may have very different functions and importance. This is clearly a possibility in different cultures or countries. It was suggested in interviews, for example, that European consultors often do have important roles to play, unlike those in the United States. Certainly the lives and duties of priests and prelates in Latin America, Africa, or Eastern Europe differ considerably from those in the United States. This is not to say that the resource dependence model cannot be applied to the Catholic church elsewhere. It does, however, suggest that much care will need to be taken in determining how to structure such a study. While research using U.S. dioceses suggests that efforts should concentrate on the parishes, dioceses facing more threatening environments may need to be studied differently. A diocese facing greater external threats might be much more unified than those studied here.[1]

The results of this research are significant in that they extend the findings of other authors whose research has suggested structured study of religious groups using models from management or marketing theory. The continuance of progress in this direction is important to the better understanding of religious organizations and may eventually provide information which is transferable to other organizations. It also appears that this progress is likely to be applicable to the study of other religious groups. However, this will require further testing.

Suggestions for Further Research

Because this is an exploratory study the possibilities for further research are almost limitless. One possibility clearly suggested in this research is to concentrate on a smaller unit of study—the parish. The case study suggested that at the parish level there tended to be more ecumenical activity. There is also reason to expect that greater concern for local community problems might be found at this level. Some aspects of parish structures, such as the existence of centrally located advisory boards—parish councils—seem to indicate that traditional resource dependence tests might be more readily adapted to these units. Findings of such a study could also be easily compared with studies at the congregational level of other faith groups, allowing the researcher to examine the impact of different hierarchical structures on resource dependence.

There are still many possibilities for continued study within the Catholic church at the diocesan level as well. It appears likely that more and more dioceses will develop pastoral councils in coming years. The official purpose of these units is to provide more input by parishioners. However, study may yield interesting insight as to other unofficial functions, including the possibility that a pastoral council may act as a linking mechanism with other community organizations.

The priests' senate was not studied in this research because it contained no "outside membership"—it is made up entirely of priests. However, given the findings which seem to indicate the location of many boundary-spanning activities at the parish level, it may be worthwhile to take a closer look at the parish priests who serve on this advisory body. The priests' senate is the closest thing to a central advisory unit that presently exists in a Roman Catholic diocese. Its study, using a resource dependence framework, might provide a better understanding of how a Catholic diocese interacts with the environment.

Studies of other dioceses, both in the United States and worldwide, could yield very interesting and valuable information. Broad organizational studies might reveal considerably different structures outside the U.S. Structural differences in dioceses in more threatening environments could provide valuable insights which may be applicable to other secular organizations facing similar stress. Even if subunits in other dioceses appear to be the same their respective functions, positions, and relative power within the diocesan hierarchy may be considerably different.

While this book studies attempts by one religious organization to exert influence on its environment through various arrangements, it would be interesting to study nonchurch organizations for evidence of the influence of religious organizations on them. This would probably be quite difficult, but a carefully planned survey of organization members similar to research done in Argentina by Miller, Chamorro, and Agulla[2] would seem to have the potential to yield much valuable information. It would also be interesting to attempt to locate important links which secular organizations might have with religious organizations (beyond simply the membership of employees in religious groups).

Clearly there are many possibilities for further study. This book highlights important channels of religious group influence. Its findings suggest that studying them as organizations may provide better understanding of these channels and, conceivably, useful information for the practicing manager. An organization as large and enduring as the Roman Catholic church must, and clearly has, developed processes which help it to better deal with, or adapt to, a wide variety of diverse environments and situations. While many of the expectations of this research were not directly confirmed, what was discovered does provide a base of useful information about the management of the Catholic church in society. It is to be hoped that this can be used to give direction to future, more informative, management study.

Appendix A

Education Letter

 INDIANA UNIVERSITY

SCHOOL OF BUSINESS
Bloomington/Indianapolis

BU 478
Bloomington, IN 47405
April, 1982

Dear Current or Past Member of the Archdiocesan Board of Education:

I am presently doing dissertation research on the Roman Catholic Church.
Much of this research centers on the Archdiocese of Indianapolis. This
research is an attempt to study the organization of one part of the Church
in an effort to gain a better understanding of its role in the community.
The Archbishop and several of the Archdiocesan Prelates will be participating
in the study. It has been approved by the current Board of Directors of
Catholic Social Services and the Archdiocesan Board of Education. The research is being done under the supervision of Dr. Richard N. Farmer, Professor of International Business.

As part of this research I am sending you a questionnaire which I hope you
will fill out and return to me in the enclosed stamped and pre-addressed
envelope. I have no interest in identifying individuals so please be assured
that your responses will be completely anonymous. If, for some reason, you
should feel that a particular question is too sensitive to answer, I would
prefer that you fill out the rest of the questionnaire and return it incomplete,
rather than not fill out any of it.

Thank you in advance for your help in this research.

Cordially,

Scott R. Safranski
Indiana University

SRS/ss

Encl.

Appendix B

Education Questionnaire

INSTRUCTIONS: Please answer the questions below by either checking the proper choice and/or filling in the blank.

1. Sex: _____M _____F

2. Ethnic Origin: _____European _____American Indian
    _____African _____Asian
    _____Hispanic _____Other--Please Specify _____

3. During what years did you serve on the Archdiocesan Board of Education:

    19_____ to 19_____

4. When elected to the board what was your occupation?_____

5. If you worked in a large company or firm, what position did you hold when first elected to the board? _____

6. Were you on an advisory board (or board of directors) for any other community or business institution when elected to the board?

    _____Yes (Please Name) _____ _____

    _____No _____ _____

7. Were you a member of other voluntary organizations at the time you were elected?

    _____Yes (Please list and give positions held)

    _____

    _____

    _____No

8. When elected to the board did you live:
    _____ In Marion County
         Township: _____Pike _____Wayne _____Decatur
         _____Washington _____Center _____Perry
         _____Lawrence _____Warren _____Franklin
    _____Outside Marion County

9. Have you ever had any training or experience in the field of education aside from your work on the Archdiocesan board?

_____Yes--Please Describe _____

_____No _____

10. What was your age when elected to the board?
    _____Under 30   _____50-59
    _____30-39   _____60-69
    _____40-49   _____70 or over

11. Do you have a college degree(s)? _____Yes   Degree_____ Major_____
                                                 Degree_____ Major_____
                                                 Degree_____ Major_____
                              _____No

Appendix C

Prestige Rating

Estimation of NORC Prestige Rating form Income and Education, for 45
Selected Occupations:

	Socio-economic Index
Accountants and auditors (accountant for a large business)	78
Airplane pilots and navigators (airline pilot)	79
Architects (architect)	90
Authors (author of novels)	76
Chemists (chemist)	79
Clergymen (minister)	52
College presidents, professors, and instructors (n.e.c.) (college professor)	84
Dentists (dentist)	96
Editors and reporters (reporter on a daily newspaper)	82
Engineers, civil (civil engineer)	84
Funeral directors and embalmers (undertaker)	59
Lawyers and judges (lawyer)	93
Physicians and surgeons (physician)	92
Social and welfare workers, except group (welfare worker for a city government)	64
Teachers (n.e.c.) (instructor in the public schools)	72
Conductors, railroad (railroad conductor)	58
Managers, officials, and proprietors (n.e.c.)- self-employed Construction (building contractor)	51
Manufacturing (owner of a factory that employes about 100 people)	61
Retail trade (manager of a small store in a city)	43
Banking and other finance (banker)	85
Bookkeepers and secretaries (bookkeeper)	51
Mail-carriers (mail carrier)	53
Insurance agents and brokers (insurance agent)	66
Salesmen and sales clerks (n.e.c.), retail trade (clerk in store)	39
Carpenters (carpenter)	19
Electricians (electrician)	44
Locomotive engineers (railroad engineer)	58

	Socio-economic Index
Machinists (trained engineer)------------------------------	33
Mechanics and repairmen, automobile (automobile repairman)-------------------------------	19
Plumbers and pipe-fitters (plumber)----------------------	34
Attendants, auto service and parking (filling-station attendant)---------------------------	19
Mine operative and laborers (n.e.c.), coal mining (coal miner)-------------------------------------	2
Motormen, street, subway and elevated railway (streetcar motorman)----------------------------	34
Taxicab-drivers and chauffeurs (taxi-driver)-------------	10
Truck and tractor-drivers (truck-driver)-----------------	15
Operatives and kindred workers (n.e.c.), Manufacturing (machine-operator in a factory)---------	17
Barbers, beauticians, and manicurists (barber)-----------	17
Bartenders (bartender)----------------------------------	19
Bootblacks (shoe-shiner)--------------------------------	8
Cooks, except private household (restaurant cook)--------	15
Counter and fountain workers (soda fountain clerk)-------	17
Guards, watchmen, and doorkeepers (night watchmen)-------	18
Janitors and sextons (janitor)--------------------------	9
Policemen and detectives, government (policeman)---------	40
Waiters and waitresses (restaurant waiter)---------------	16

Source: Reiss, Albert J., Jr; Duncan, Otis Dudley, Matt, Paul K.;
          and North, Cecil C. Occupations and Social Status.
          New York: The Free Press of Glencoe, Inc., 1961.

Appendix D

Organization Coding System

--Roman Catholic Church Units and Organizations (100-199)

    (100-129)   Archdiocesan Structures
    (130-159)   Parish and Deanery Structures
    (160-199)   General Organizations (KC, NCCM, etc.)

--Government Units/Offices, Educational Institutions and Related Professional
  and Supportive Associations, Communications Firms, and Related Professional
  Associations, Labor Organizations (200-299)

    (200-230)   Government Units
    (231-240)   Utilities
    (241-260)   Educational Institutions and Boards of Education
    (261-280)   Professional Education Associations, Academic Societies
              and Editorial Boards
    (281-290)   Communications Firms and Related Professional Associations
    (291-299)   Labor Organizations

--Law Firms and Related Professional Associaitons (300-399)

    (300-330)   Law Firms
    (331-399)   Professional Associations (Organized low numbers to
              high numbers: Judges' Associations, Inter-national
              Law Associations, National, State, Local, Professional
              Fraternities, Civic Legal Support Groups)

--Business and Real Estate Firms and Related Professional Associations (400-499)

    (400-415)   Real Estate and Architectural Firms
    (416-424)   Real Estate and Architectural Professional Associations
    (425-445)   Manufacturing Firms
    (446-460)   Service Firms (Transportation, Accountants, Funeral, etc.)
    (461-470)   Restaurant and Retail
    (471-484)   Trade Specific Associations
    (485-499)   Public Service Associations (B.B.B., C. of C., etc.)
              and Businessmen's Clubs (Rotary,etc.)

--Financial Businesses, Insurance Firms, Related Associations (500-599)

    (500-530) Banks, Credit Unions, S & L's, Investment Companies,
              Investor Services
    (531-569) Insurance Firms
    (570-599) Professional Associations

--Medical Care and Retirement Facilities, Supportive Community Associations,
  Related Professional Associations (600-699)

      (600-605) County Health Corporations
      (606-615) Hospitals
      (616-630) Clinics
      (631-640) Retirement Homes
      (641-649) Personal Practice
      (650-659) Professional Organizations
      (660-669) Hospital Support Groups
      (670-679) Civic Health Care Planning Agencies
      (680-699) Illness Concern Groups (Heart Association, etc.)

--Community Service Organizations, Social Service Organizations, Special
  Interest Organizations, Youth Organizations (700-799)

      (700-732) Community Service Organizations
      (733-770) Social Service Organizations
      (771-791) Special Interest Organizations (NAACP, etc.)
      (792-799) Youth Organizations

--Social Clubs, Athletic Clubs, Country Clubs, Fraternal Organizations,
  College and Alumni Organizations (800-899)

      (800-815) College and Alumni Organizations
      (816-825) Fraternal Organizations
      (826-899) Social Clubs (General and Special Interest), Athletic
                Clubs, Country Clubs, Neighborhood Associations

Appendix E

Correlations among Variables

CORRELATIONS AMONG VARIABLES IN DISCRIMINANT ANALYSIS
OF BOARD MEMBERS

	Var. 3	N Boards	C Boards	C Orgs	Var. 59
Var. 3	1.0000				
	P=******				
N Boards	- .0959	1.0000			
	P= .154	P=******			
C Boards	.0443	.1324	1.0000		
	P= .319	P= .077	P=******		
C Orgs	.1203	.0842	.1220	1.0000	
	P= .100	P= .184	P= .095	P=******	
Var. 59	.1178	- .0817	.0027	.0496	1.0000
	P= .107	P= .193	P= .489	P= .299	P=******
Var. 7	.0742	.1923	- .2626	- .0042	- .0691
	P= .231	P= .026	P= .004	P= .483	P= .246
N Orgs	.0594	.6990	- .0421	.1165	.0140
	P= .264	P= .001	P= .326	P= .105	P= .441
Var. 58	.0632	.0830	- .0041	.0667	.2129
	P= .251	P= .187	P= .482	P= .238	P= .011
Educt	- .0877	.1621	- .0510	- .1021	- .1894
	P= .176	P= .040	P= .292	P= .137	P= .021

	Var. 7	N Orgs	Var. 58	Educt
Var. 3				
N Boards				
C Boards				
C Orgs				
Var. 59				
Var. 7	1.0000			
	P=******			

	Var. 7	N Orgs	Var. 58	Educt
N Orgs	.2722	1.0000		
	P= .003	P=******		
Var. 58	.0995	.0434	1.0000	
	P= .159	P= .321	P=******	
Educt	.4342	.1751	- .4075	1.0000
	P= .001	P= .030	P= .001	P=******

Appendix F

Board of Social Services Agency Size Data

YEAR	TOTAL EXPENSES (Thousands of Dollars)	TOTAL AGENCY CLIENTS SERVED
1981	593	6090
1980	518	6100
1979	441	5636
1978	407	5010
1977	365	4558
1976	384	3954
1975	356	4006
1974	362	NA
1973	356	NA
1972	392	NA
1971	422	NA
1970	400	NA
1969	364	NA
1968	NA	NA
1967	418	NA
1966	417	NA
1965	363	NA

Appendix G

School Enrollment

YEAR BEGINNING	ELEMENTARY	SECONDARY	TOTAL
Sept. 1965	34142	8317	42459
Sept. 1966	33062	8049	41111
Sept. 1967	32162	8080	40242
Sept. 1968	30526	7677	38203
Sept. 1969	27961	7218	35179
Sept. 1970	24955	7218	32173
Sept. 1971	23481	6346	29827
Sept. 1972	21517	6257	27774
Sept. 1973	20545	6391	26936
Sept. 1974	19667	6433	26100
Sept. 1975	18771	6289	25060
Sept. 1976	18173	6104	24277
Sept. 1977	17450	5703	23153
Sept. 1978	17134	5610	22744
Sept. 1979	16701	5464	22165
Sept. 1980	16546	5324	21870
Sept. 1981	16772	5236	22008

Appendix H

Board Members from Minority Groups

SOCIAL SERVICES MEMBERS FROM MINORITY GROUPS --
YEAR JOINED BOARD

YEAR	ABSOLUTE FREQ	RELATIVE FREQ (PCT)	ADJUSTED FREQ (PCT)	CUM FREQ (PCT)
1970	1	12.5	14.5	14.3
1971	1	12.5	14.3	28.6
1979	2	25.0	28.6	57.1
1980	1	12.5	14.3	71.4
1981	1	12.5	14.3	85.7
1982	1	12.5	14.3	100.0
Year Unknown	1	12.5		
TOTAL	8	100.0	100.0	

EDUCATION MEMBERS FROM MINORITY GROUPS
YEAR JOINED BOARD

YEAR	ABSOLUTE FREQ	RELATIVE FREQ (PCT)	ADJUSTED FREQ (PCT)	CUM FREQ (PCT)
1960	1	33.3	33.3	33.3
1970	1	33.3	33.3	66.7
1977	1	33.3	33.3	100.0
TOTAL	3	100.0	100.0	

Appendix I

National Cover Letter

 INDIANA UNIVERSITY

SCHOOL OF BUSINESS
Bloomington/Indianapolis

BU 478
Bloomington, IN 47405
June 7, 1982

Dear Father

I am doing dissertation research under the direction of Professor Richard Farmer as part of the requirements for the completion of a Doctor of Business Administration Degree. The goal of this research is to study the organization of the Roman Catholic Church on a diocesan level and the role the Church plays in the community and nation. An earlier study concentrated on the Archdiocese of Indianapolis and included analysis of some diocesan records as well as extensive interviews with several diocesan officals. In an attempt to see if what I have learned can be generalized to other dioceses I am now sending a questionnaire to the Vicar General or Chancellor of every diocese in the United States. You will find a copy of this survey enclosed.

If you could find the time to fill out the attached survey it would provide a valuable addition to this reserach. While the questionnaire asks a large number of rather detailed and difficult questions I realize that you are very busy and cannot take the time to pull exact answers out of your files. I would simply ask that you record your _impressions_ or _educated estimates_ of the best answers (even where statistics are called for). You may be assured that your responses will be kept completely anonymous. If you would be interested in a report of the results of this survey please follow the instructions on the cover page of the questionnaire.

Thank you in advance for your cooperation.

Sincerely,

Scott R. Safranski
International Business

Appendix J

National Survey Questionnaire

DIRECTIONS: Please answer the following questions by either filling in the blank or circling the correct number. Please keep in mind that we are interested in your impressions. We know that you are very busy and do not expect you to look up exact answers.

1:5   What, in your opinion, is the single most important issue facing the Catholic Church on a national level in the 1980s?

_____

_____

_____

_____

1:7   What, in your opinion, is the single most important issue facing the Catholic Church on an international level in the 1980s?

_____

_____

_____

_____

1:9   What, in your opinion, is the single most important issue facing your diocese in the 1980s?

_____

_____

_____

_____

1:11   How often does the ordinary travel to Washington for the purpose of meeting with members of the Apostolic Delegation? (please circle one)

       1. At least once a year
       2. At least once every two years
       3. At least once every three years
       4. At least once every four years
       5. At least once every five years (or less)

1:12   How often does the ordinary travel to Rome for the purpose of meeting with members of the Sacred Congregations or with the Pope? (please circle one)

       1. At least once a year
       2. At least once every two years
       3. At least once every three years
       4. At least once every four years
       5. At least once every five years (or less)

1:13   How frequently does the ordinary meet with other bishops of the province as as a group? (please circle one)

       1. At least four times per year
       2. At least three times per year
       3. At least two times per year
       4. At least one time per year
       5. Less than one time per year

To what extent do issues of social concern (e.g., capital punishment, nuclear disarmament, human equality issues, etc.) arise in your diocese with: (please circle one on each line)

		Not at all				To a great extent
1:14	The oridinary	1	2	3	4	5
1:15	The priests' senate	1	2	3	4	5
1:16	The pastoral council	1	2	3	4	5
1:17	Women Religious	1	2	3	4	5
1:18	Men Religious	1	2	3	4	5
1:19	Individual priests	1	2	3	4	5
1:20	Individual lay people	1	2	3	4	5
1:21	The state and/or U.S. Catholic Conference	1	2	3	4	5

To what extent do issues of economic concern (e.g., corporate corruption, treatment of labor, treatment of migrant workers or tenant farmers, etc.) arise in your diocese with: (please circle one on each line)

1:22	The ordinary	1	2	3	4	5
1:23	The priests' senate	1	2	3	4	5
1:24	The pastoral council	1	2	3	4	5
1:25	Women Religious	1	2	3	4	5
1:26	Men Religious	1	2	3	4	5
1:27	Individual priests	1	2	3	4	5
1:28	Individual lay people	1	2	3	4	5
1:29	The state and/or U.S. Catholic Conference	1	2	3	4	5

To what extent do the following organizations within the
Church provide information on world events of concern
(e.g., Poland, El Salvadore, etc.)? (please circle one
on each line)

		Not at all				To a great extent
1:30	The National Conference of Catholic Bishops	1	2	3	4	5
1:31	The National Federation of Priests' Councils	1	2	3	4	5
1:32	The Apostolic Delegation	1	2	3	4	5
1:33	The State and/or U.S. Catholic Conference	1	2	3	4	5

To what extent do the following organizations within the
Church provide information on national events of concern
(e.g., Human Rights, Abortion vs. Pro-life, etc.)? (please
circle one on each line)

1:34	The National Conference on Catholic Bishops	1	2	3	4	5
1:35	The National Federation of Priests' Councils	1	2	3	4	5
1:36	The Apostolic Delegation	1	2	3	4	5
1:37	The State and/or U.S. Catholic Conference	1	2	3	4	5

To what extent do the following organizations within the
Church provide information on local events of concern?
(please circle one on each line)

1:38	The National Conference of Catholic Bishops	1	2	3	4	5
1:39	The National Federation of Priests' Councils	1	2	3	4	5
1:40	The Apostolic Delegation	1	2	3	4	5
1:41	The State and/or U.S. Catholic Conference	1	2	3	4	5

1:42	To what extent is the current ordinary active in national bishops' organizations such as the NCCB?	1	2	3	4	5
1:43	To what extent was the previous ordinary active in national bishops' organizations such as the NCCB?	1	2	3	4	5
1:44	To what extent is the Church's hierarchy (e.g., the Apostolic Delegation, the Vatican) consulted by the diocese as it researches a problem and determines a course of action?	1	2	3	4	5
1:45	To what extent are other units of the Church (e.g., other dioceses) consulted by your diocese as it researches a problem and determines a course of action?	1	2	3	4	5
1:46	To what extent is the current ordinary supportive of agents of the diocese (clergy, etc.) actively taking a position on issues of social concern?	1	2	3	4	5
1:47	To what extent was the previous ordinary supportive of agents of the diocese (clergy, etc.) actively taking a position on local issues of social concern?	1	2	3	4	5

1:48   To what extent does the diocese work with or through government agencies to offer such things as community education programs on drug abuse, alcohol abuse, human equality, etc.?   Not at all   To a great extent
         1   2   3   4   5

1:49   To what extent does the diocese work with or through business organizations to offer such tings as community education programs on drug abuse, alcohol abuse, human equality, etc.?   1   2   3   4   5

1:50   To what extent is the current ordinary active in the local community (e.g., on community boards and commissions, active in various areas of community concern)?   1   2   3   4   5

1:51   To what extent was the previous ordinary active in the local community (e.g., on community boards and commissions, active in various areas of community concern)?   1   2   3   4   5

1:52   To what extent does the current ordinary travel to visit individual parishes in the diocese?   1   2   3   4   5

1:53   To what extent did the previous ordinary travel to visit individual parishes in the diocese?   1   2   3   4   5

1:54   To what extent do individual parishes have a voice in the major decisions of the diocese?   1   2   3   4   5

1:55   To what extent are the parishes of the diocese in a state of harmony on local issues facing the diocese?   1   2   3   4   5

1:56   To what extent are the priests in the diocese aware of the existence of the Priests' Senate?   1   2   3   4   5

1:57   To what extent have the priests in the diocese been able to use the Priests' Senate to express their concerns?   1   2   3   4   5

1:58   To what extent does the diocese as a whole join forces with other major faiths in the community (e.g., Lutheran, Methodist, Presbyterian, Jewish, etc.) in addressing issues of local concern?   1   2   3   4   5

1:59   What percentage of diocesan clergy are active in local ministerial organiza- tions (local groups of ministers from various denominations who meet to address issues of concern in their area)? (please circle one)

       1.   0-20%
       2.   21-40%
       3.   41-60%
       4.   61-80%
       5.   81-100%

1:60   Is the diocese a member of any community-wide ecumenical organizations (such as a council of churches) on a long-term basis? (please circle one)

       1.   Yes--Year diocese first joined such an organization: _____
       2.   No

1:61 What portion of the parishes in the diocese have parish councils? (please circle one)

    1. 0-20%
    2. 21-40%
    3. 41-60%
    4. 61-80%
    5. 81-100%

1:62 Is there, currently, a working pastoral council in the diocese? (please circle one)

    1. Yes
    2. No

To what extent would the following qualities be important in a lay person serving on a pastoral council? (please circle one on each line)

	Not at all				To a great extent
1:63 Active in parish organizations	1	2	3	4	5
1:64 Active in non-church community organizations	1	2	3	4	5
1:65 Have a knowledge of the organization of the diocese	1	2	3	4	5
1:66 Have experience in other diocesan-wide committees and activities	1	2	3	4	5
1:67 Be able to represent specific groups and/or current concerns of the community	1	2	3	4	5

1:68 To what extent does the present ordinary support the existence (or future formation) of a pastoral council?   1 2 3 4 5

To what extent would the following characteristics be required of a bishop to serve successfully as ordinary of your diocese? (please circle one on each line)

1:69 Be a biblical scholar	1	2	3	4	5
1:70 Be a temporal scholar	1	2	3	4	5
1:71 Personal charm or charisma	1	2	3	4	5
1:72 Ability to empathize with individual problems	1	2	3	4	5
1:73 Be "an organizer"	1	2	3	4	5
1:74 Be proficient at establishing contacts in the local community	1	2	3	4	5
1:75 Already have contacts in the local community	1	2	3	4	5
1:76 Sensitivity to the concerns of specific groups in the diocese	1	2	3	4	5

1:77 What portion of the total population in the area of your diocese is Catholic? (please circle one)

    1.   0-10%   6. 51-60%
    2. 11-20%   7. 61-70%
    3. 21-30%   8. 71-80%
    4. 31-40%   9. 81-90%
    5. 41-50%   10. 91-100%

1:78   What percentage of the diocese's operating income is obtained from the parishes in the diocese through the general collection? (please circle one).

     1.   0-20%
     2.   21-40%
     3.   41-60%
     4.   61-80%
     5.   81-100%

1:79   What percentage of the diocese's operating income is obtained from sources outside the diocese such as the gifts of organizations? (please circle one)

     1.   0-20%
     2.   21-40%
     3.   41-60%
     4.   61-80%
     5.   81-100%

1:80   What percentage of the diocese's operating income is obtained from rents on lands and properties owned by the diocese? (please circle one)

     1.   0-20%
     2.   21-40%
     3.   41-60%
     4.   61-80%
     5.   81-100%

2:5   What percentage of the diocese's operating income is obtained from returns on stocks and similar investments? (please circle one)

     1.   0-20%
     2.   21-40%
     3.   41-60%
     4.   61-80%
     5.   81-100%

To what extent does the diocese invest excess funds (when it has them in: (please circle one on each line)

	Not at all				To a great extent
2:6 A bank savings account	1	2	3	4	5
2:7 Bonds	1	2	3	4	5
2:8 Stocks	1	2	3	4	5
2:9 Property	1	2	3	4	5
2:10 Lend to individual parishes	1	2	3	4	5
2:11 Lend to other dioceses	1	2	3	4	5
2:12 Lend to Church hierarchy	1	2	3	4	5

2:13   What percentage of Catholic elementary school children in your diocese are enrolled in Catholic primary schools (K-8)? (please circle one)

     1.   0-20%
     2.   21-40%
     3.   41-60%
     4.   61-80%
     5.   81-100%

2:14   What percentage of the <u>public</u> board of education in your community is made up of Catholics? (please circle one)

    1. 0-20%
    2. 21-40%
    3. 41-60%
    4. 61-80%
    5. 81-100%

2:15   Does your diocese have a diocesan-wide Board of Catholic Education (please circle one)
    1. Yes--over 50% are lay people
    2. Yes--about 50% are lay people and 50% are clergy/religious
    3. Yes--over 50% are clergy/religious
    4. No--there is no diocesan-wide Board of Catholic Education

<u>If</u> <u>yes</u>--please continue
<u>If</u> <u>no</u>--please go to top of next page

To what extent would the following qualities be important in a lay person serving on the diocesan Board of Catholic Education? (Not at all ... To a great extent)

2:16   Active in parish organizations   1 2 3 4 5
2:17   Active in non-Church community organizations   1 2 3 4 5
2:18   Have experience in other diocesan-wide committees and activities   1 2 3 4 5
2:19   Are affiliated with other educators in the community   1 2 3 4 5
2:20   Are affiliated with important groups in the community   1 2 3 4 5
2:21   Have knowledge and/or experience in the field of education   1 2 3 4 5

2:22   To what extent are the expenses of the diocesan schools covered by tuition? (please circle one)

    1. 0-20%
    2. 21-40%
    3. 41-60%
    4. 61-80%
    5. 81-100%

2:23   To what extent are the expenses of the diocesan schools covered by contributions directly from individual parishes? (please check one)

    1. 0-20%
    2. 21-40%
    3. 41-60%
    4. 61-80%
    5. 81-100%

2:24   To what extent are the expenses of the diocesan schools covered by funds allocated by the diocese? (please circle one)

    1. 0-20%
    2. 21-40%
    3. 41-60%
    4. 61-80%
    5. 81-100%

2:25   Does the diocese have a board of directors of Catholic Social Services (or
       of Catholic Charities)?   (please circle one)

     1.   Yes--over 50% are lay people
     2.   Yes--about 50% are lay people and 50% are clergy/religious
     3.   Yes--over 50% are clergy/religious
     4.   No--the diocese does not have a board of directors of Catholic
          Social Services (or of Catholic charities)

If yes--please continue
If no--please go to bottom of last page.

To what extent would the following qualities be important
in a lay person serving on a board of directors of Cath-   Not   To a
olic Social Services? (please circle one on each line)   at   great
                                              all   extent

		Not at all				To a great extent
2:26	Active in parish organizations	1	2	3	4	5
2:27	Active in non-church community organizations	1	2	3	4	5
2:28	Have experience in other diocesan-wide committees and activities	1	2	3	4	5
2:29	Are affiliated with other social-service organizations	1	2	3	4	5
2:30	Are affiliated with important groups in the community	1	2	3	4	5
2:31	Have knowledge and/or experience in the field of social work	1	2	3	4	5

2:32   To what extent are the expenses of Catholic Social Services covered by funds
       contributed directly by parishes?   (please circle one)
     1.   0-20%
     2.   21-40%
     3.   41-60%
     4.   61-80%
     5.   81-100%

2:33   To what extent are the expenses of Catholic Social Services covered by funds
       allocated by the diocese?   (please circle one)

     1.   0-20%
     2.   21-40%
     3.   41-60%
     4.   61-80%
     5.   81-100%

2:34   To what extent are the expenses of Catholic Social Services covered by funds
       from the United Way and similar agencies?   (please circle one)

     1.   0-20%
     2.   21-40%
     3.   41-60%
     4.   61-80%
     5.   81-100%

2:35   To what extent are the expenses of Catholic Social Services covered by fees
        charged for services? (please circle one)

            1.   0-20%
            2.   21-40%
            3.   41-60%
            4.   61-80%
            5.   81-100%

2:36   To what extent are the expenses of Catholic Social Services covered by
        government support such as Federal Counseling Fees? (please circle one)

            1.   0-20%
            2.   21-40%
            3.   41-60%
            4.   61-80%
            5.   81-100%

2:37   To what extent are the expenses of Catholic Social Services covered by
        direct contributions from business organizations in the community?
        (please circle one)

            1.   0-20%
            2.   21-40%
            3.   41-60%
            4.   61-80%
            5.   81-100%

I would appreciate any comments you might have on this questionnaire or on individual
questions. Please feel free to write them in the space below. Thank you for your
time in filling out this survey!

Appendix K

Results of National Survey

RESULTS OF NATIONAL SURVEY
OF ROMAN CATHOLIC DIOCESES

(Results of questionnaire broken down by percent of the total population in each diocese which is Catholic -- see Item 70)

The concerns or issues listed below provide a summarization of concerns which were brought up by respondents to the questionnaire in answer to the first three items. The code numbers shown were arbitrarily assigned in an attempt to categorize or rank the concerns. Low numbers were assigned to those which appeared to represent an inward (Church concern) orientation while high numbers were assigned to those which appeared to represent an outward (concern with world events, economy, etc.) orientation.

Concern	Code
Accountability	14
Church Unity	02
Clergy Personnel	12
Disarmament/Peace	54
Drug Problems	48
Economy (& Implications for the Church)	50
Ecumenism	40
Educating Catholic Laity in the Basics of Faith	04
Evangelization & Spiritual Renewal (Updating Church Ministries)	16
Human Dignity Issues	44
Lay Ministries & Lay Participation in the Church	28
Marriage & Family Issues	36
Ministering to Individual Needs & Concerns	32
Peace & Justice Issues	56
Preserving Catholic Schools	08
Quality of Life & Problems of Population & Crowding	52
Strengthening Faith & Morals	06
Translating Teachings of Vatican II into Practice	24
Validity of Byzantine Church	10

1. What, in your opinion, is the single most important issue facing the Catholic Church on a <u>national level</u> in the 1980s?

Concern	Code	Frequencies
Evangelization & Spiritual Renewal (Updating Church Ministries)	16	15
Marriage & Family Issues	12	10
Disarmament/Peace	54	7
Lay Ministries & Lay Participation in the Church	28	6
Strengthening Faith & Morals	06	5
Peace & Justice Issues	56	5
Educating Catholic Laity in the Basics of Faith	04	3
Translating Vatican II into Practice	24	3
Human Dignity Issues	44	3
Ministering to Individual Needs & Concerns	32	2
Economy (& Implications for the Church)	50	2
Church Unity	02	1
Accountability	14	1
Drug Problems	48	1
Quality of Life & Problems of Population & Crowding	52	1
No response	09	6

2. What, in your opinion, is the single most important issue facing the Catholic Church on an <u>international level</u> in the 1980s?

Concern	Code	Frequencies
Peace & Justice Issues	56	22
Disarmament/Peace	54	13
Evangelization & Spiritual Renewal (Updating Church Ministries)	16	7
Human Dignity Issues	44	7
Clergy Personnel	12	6
Church Unity	02	5
Strengthening Faith & Morals	06	3
Marriage & Family Issues	36	3
Lay Ministries & Lay Participation in the Church	28	2
Ecumenism	40	2
Accountability	14	1
Translating Teachings of Vatican II into Practice	24	1
Ministering to Individual Needs & Concerns	32	1
No response	09	6

3. What, in your opinion, is the single most important issue facing your diocese in the 1980s?

Concern	Code	Frequencies
Clergy Personnel	12	23
Evangelization & Spiritual Renewal (Updating Church Ministries)	16	14
Lay Ministries & Lay Participation in the Church	28	8
Marriage & Family Issues	36	5
Church Unity	02	4
Preserving Catholic Schools	08	3
Translating Teachings of Vatican II into Practice	24	3
Peace & Justice Issues	56	3
Educating Cathlic Laity in the Basics of Faith	04	2
Human Dignity Issues	44	2
Quality of Life & Problems of Population & Crowding	52	2
Strengthening Faith & Morals	06	1
Validity of Byzantine Church	10	1
Accountability	14	1
Ministering to Individual Needs & Concerns	32	1
Disarmament/Peace	54	5
No response	09	5

4. How often does the ordinary travel to Washington for the purpose of meeting with members of the Apostolic Delegation?

1. At least once a year
2. At least once every two years
3. At least once every three years
4. At least once every four years
5. At least once every five years
9. No response

FREQUENCIES:	General Population	1-10%	11-20%	21-30%	31-40%	41-50%
1.	24	6	4	7	3	1
2.	2	--	1	--	1	--
3.	2	1	--	--	1	--
4.	2	--	--	--	1	--
5.	39	9	10	7	3	5
9.	10	3	3	1	3	--
MEAN:	3.471	3.375	3.733	3.000	3.300	4.333
MEDIAN:	4.628	4.222	4.750	3.000	3.500	4.600
MODE:	5.000	5.000	5.000	1.000	1.000	5.000
STD. DEV.:	1.901	1.962	1.870	2.075	1.947	1.633

5. How often does the ordinary travel to Rome for the purpose of meeting with members of the Sacred Congregations or with the Pope?

1. At least once a year	4. At least once every four years
2. At least once every two years	5. At least once every five years
3. At least once every three years	9. No response

FREQUENCIES:	General Population	1-10%	11-20%	21-30%	31-40%	41-50%
1.	4	--	1	2	--	--
2.	3	--	--	--	1	1
3.	4	--	--	--	2	--
4.	3	1	1	1	--	--
5.	63	17	15	12	9	5
9.	2	1	1	--	--	--
MEAN:	4.532	4.944	4.706	4.400	4.417	4.500
MEDIAN:	4.889	4.971	4.933	4.875	4.833	4.700
MODE	5.000	5.000	5.000	5.000	5.000	5.000
STD. DEV.:	1.107	.236	.985	1.404	1.084	1.225

6. How frequently does the ordinary meet with other bishops of the province as a group?

1. At least four times per year	4. At least one time per year
2. At least three times per year	5. Less than one time per year
3. At least two times per year	9. No response

FREQUENCIES:	General Population	1-10%	11-20%	21-30%	31-40%	41-50%
1.	33	4	7	3	8	5
2.	11	3	1	6	--	1
3.	19	7	6	2	2	--
4.	12	3	4	2	2	--
5.	3	1	--	2	--	--
9.	1	1	--	--	--	--
MEAN:	2.244	2.667	2.389	2.600	1.833	1.167
MEDIAN:	2.045	2.786	2.667	2.250	1.250	1.100
MODE:	1.000	3.000	1.000	2.000	1.000	1.000
STD. DEV.:	1.261	1.188	1.243	1.352	1.267	.408

UNLESS OTHERWISE INDICATED, the following values apply to responses indicated below:

1	2	3	4	5		9
Not at all				To a great extent		No response

NOTE: The following question applies to #'s 7-14 below. "To what extent do issues of <u>social concern</u> (e.g., capital punishment, nuclear disarmament, human equality issues, etc.) arise in your diocese with:"

7. The ordinary

FREQUENCIES:	General Population	1-10%	11-20%	21-30%	31-40%	41-50%
1.	--	--	--	--	--	--
2.	5	--	2	2	1	--
3.	16	4	2	2	4	1
4.	23	6	3	6	3	2
5.	34	8	11	5	4	3
9.	1	1	--	--	--	--
MEAN:	4.103	4.222	4.278	3.933	3.833	4.333
MEDIAN:	4.283	4.333	4.682	4.083	3.833	4.500
MODE:	5.000	5.000	5.000	4.000	3.000	5.000
STD. DEV.:	.948	.808	1.074	1.033	1.030	.816

8. The priests' senate

FREQUENCIES:	General Population	1-10%	11-20%	21-30%	31-40%	41-50%
1.	2	--	--	1	--	--
2.	9	4	--	2	3	--
3.	28	3	8	5	4	3
4.	25	7	7	5	3	1
5.	13	3	3	2	2	2
9.	2	2	--	--	--	--
MEAN:	3.494	3.529	3.722	3.333	3.333	3.833
MEDIAN:	3.482	3.714	3.643	3.400	3.250	3.500
MODE:	3.000	4.000	3.000	3.000	3.000	3.000
STD. DEV.:	.995	1.068	.752	1.113	1.073	.983

9. The pastoral council

FREQUENCIES:	General Population	1-10%	11-20%	21-30%	31-40%	41-50%
1.	12	3	1	3	3	1
2.	12	1	2	4	3	1
3.	21	5	7	2	2	2
4.	9	3	4	1	1	--
5.	5	1	1	1	1	--
9.	20	6	3	4	2	2
MEAN:	2.712	2.846	3.133	2.364	2.400	2.250
MEDIAN:	2.762	3.000	3.143	2.125	2.167	2.250
MODE:	3.000	3.000	3.000	2.000	1.000	3.000
STD. DEV.:	1.204	1.281	.990	1.286	1.350	.957

10. Women Religious

FREQUENCIES:	General Population	1-10%	11-20%	21-30%	31-40%	41-50%
1.	1	--	--	--	--	--
2.	8	4	1	1	--	--
3.	18	3	6	7	2	--
4.	29	7	6	6	5	1
5.	20	4	5	1	4	5
9.	3	1	--	--	1	--
MEAN:	3.776	3.611	3.833	3.467	4.182	4.833
MEDIAN:	3.879	3.786	3.833	3.429	4.200	4.900
MODE:	4.000	4.000	3.000	3.000	4.000	5.000
STD. DEV.:	1.001	1.092	.924	.743	.751	.408

11. Men Religious

FREQUENCIES:	General Population	1-10%	11-20%	21-30%	31-40%	41-50%
1.	6	1	2	2	--	--
2.	14	3	3	3	2	--
3.	28	7	5	7	3	2
4.	15	3	2	2	4	4
5.	8	2	3	1	1	--
9.	8	3	3	--	2	--
MEAN:	3.070	3.125	3.067	2.800	3.400	3.667
MEDIAN:	3.054	3.071	3.000	2.857	3.500	3.750
MODE:	3.000	3.000	3.000	3.000	4.000	4.000
STD. DEV.:	1.100	1.088	1.335	1.082	.966	.516

12. Individual priests

FREQUENCIES:	General Population	1-10%	11-20%	21-30%	31-40%	41-50%
1.	--	--	--	--	--	--
2.	21	4	6	4	1	1
3.	32	7	4	8	7	3
4.	17	7	4	2	2	1
5.	7	--	4	1	1	1
9.	2	1	--	--	1	--
MEAN:	3.130	3.167	3.333	3.000	3.273	3.333
MEDIAN:	3.047	3.214	3.250	2.938	3.143	3.167
MODE:	3.000	3.000	2.000	3.000	3.000	3.000
STD. DEV.:	.923	.786	1.188	.845	.786	1.033

13. Individual lay people

FREQUENCIES:	General Population	1-10%	11-20%	21-30%	31-40%	41-50%
1.	3	--	2	--	1	--
2.	30	7	6	5	6	1
3.	32	8	6	7	3	5
4.	7	2	2	2	1	--
5.	5	1	2	1	1	--
9.	2	1	--	--	--	--
MEAN:	2.753	2.833	2.778	2.933	2.583	2.833
MEDIAN:	2.672	2.750	2.667	2.857	2.333	2.900
MODE:	3.000	3.000	2.000	3.000	2.000	3.000
STD. DEV.:	.920	.857	1.166	.884	1.084	.408

14. The state and/or U.S. Catholic Conference

FREQUENCIES:	General Population	1-10%	11-20%	21-30%	31-40%	41-50%
1.	--	--	--	--	--	--
2.	6	1	1	2	1	--
3.	19	4	6	4	2	--
4.	25	6	4	7	3	3
5.	23	4	7	1	6	3
9.	6	4	--	1	--	--
MEAN:	3.890	3.867	3.944	3.500	4.167	4.500
MEDIAN:	3.960	3.917	4.000	3.643	4.500	4.500
MODE:	4.000	4.000	5.000	4.000	5.000	4.000
STD. DEV.:	.951	.915	.998	.855	1.030	.548

NOTE: The following question applies to #'s 15-22 below. "To what extent do
issues of economic concern (e.g., corporate corruption, treatment of labor,
treatment of migrant workers or tenant farmers, etc.) arise in your diocese
with:"

15. The ordinary

FREQUENCIES:	General Population	1-10%	11-20%	21-30%	31-40%	41-50%
1.	1	--	--	--	1	--
2.	8	2	3	2	--	1
3.	24	3	4	4	5	2
4.	28	8	4	8	5	2
5.	17	5	7	1	1	1
9.	1	1	--	--	--	--
MEAN:	3.667	3.889	3.833	3.533	3.417	3.500
MEDIAN:	3.714	4.000	4.000	3.688	3.500	3.500
MODE:	4.000	4.000	5.000	4.000	3.000	3.000
STD. DEV.:	.976	.963	1.150	.834	.996	1.049

16. The priests' senate

FREQUENCIES:	General Population	1-10%	11-20%	21-30%	31-40%	41-50%
1.	2	--	--	1	1	--
2.	18	4	4	3	4	1
3.	39	8	9	9	5	3
4.	13	4	4	1	2	2
5.	4	1	1	1	--	--
9.	3	2	--	--	--	--
MEAN:	2.987	3.118	3.111	2.867	2.667	3.167
MEDIAN:	2.962	3.063	3.056	2.889	2.700	3.167
MODE:	3.000	3.000	3.000	3.000	3.000	3.000
STD. DEV.:	.856	.857	.832	.915	.888	.753

17. The pastoral council

FREQUENCIES:	General Population	1-10%	11-20%	21-30%	31-40%	41-50%
1.	15	4	2	4	4	1
2.	17	2	5	3	3	2
3.	18	4	5	4	2	1
4.	5	3	1	1	--	--
5.	3	1	1	--	--	--
9.	21	5	4	3	3	2
MEAN:	2.379	2.643	2.571	2.167	1.778	2.000
MEDIAN:	2.324	2.750	2.500	2.167	1.667	2.000
MODE:	3.000	1.000	2.000	1.000	1.000	2.000
STD. DEV.:	1.121	1.336	1.089	1.030	.833	.816

18. Women Religious

FREQUENCIES:	General Population	1-10%	11-20%	21-30%	31-40%	41-50%
1.	4	2	1	--	1	--
2.	14	4	5	3	--	--
3.	25	5	5	7	4	2
4.	23	4	5	5	4	2
5.	10	3	2	--	2	2
9.	3	1	--	--	1	--
MEAN:	3.276	3.111	3.111	3.133	3.545	4.000
MEDIAN:	3.300	3.100	3.100	3.143	3.625	4.000
MODE:	3.000	3.000	2.000	3.000	3.000	3.000
STD. DEV.:	1.078	1.278	1.132	.743	1.128	.894

19. Men Religious

FREQUENCIES:	General Population	1-10%	11-20%	21-30%	31-40%	41-50%
1.	9	2	4	2	1	--
2.	18	5	5	2	3	--
3.	28	6	3	9	3	4
4.	11	3	1	2	2	2
5.	4	1	2	--	1	--
9.	9	2	3	--	2	--
MEAN:	2.757	2.765	2.467	2.733	2.900	3.333
MEDIAN:	2.786	2.750	2.200	2.889	2.833	3.250
MODE:	3.000	3.000	2.000	3.000	2.000	3.000
STD. DEV.:	1.055	1.091	1.356	.884	1.197	.515

20. Individual priests

FREQUENCIES:	General Population	1-10%	11-20%	21-30%	31-40%	41-50%
1.	3	--	2	--	--	--
2.	22	6	5	6	2	--
3.	33	7	7	5	8	3
4.	15	3	2	3	2	3
5.	5	2	2	1	--	--
9.	1	1	--	--	--	--
MEAN:	2.962	3.056	2.833	2.933	3.000	3.500
MEDIAN:	2.924	2.929	2.786	2.800	3.000	3.500
MODE:	3.000	3.000	3.000	2.000	3.000	3.000
STD. DEV.:	.946	.998	1.150	.961	.603	.548

21. Individual lay people

FREQUENCIES:	General Population	1-10%	11-20%	21-30%	31-40%	41-50%
1.	4	--	2	--	2	--
2.	36	6	10	6	5	3
3.	27	8	4	8	1	3
4.	8	3	1	1	3	--
5.	2	1	1	--	--	--
9.	2	1	--	--	1	--
MEAN:	2.584	2.944	2.389	2.667	2.455	2.500
MEDIAN:	2.458	2.875	2.200	2.688	2.200	2.500
MODE:	2.000	3.000	2.000	3.000	2.000	2.000
STD. DEV.:	.848	.873	.979	.617	1.128	.548

22. The state and/or U.S. Catholic Conference

FREQUENCIES:	General Population	1-10%	11-20%	21-30%	31-40%	41-50%
1.	--	--	--	--	--	--
2.	10	3	1	2	3	--
3.	24	5	7	4	2	1
4.	29	4	6	7	6	4
5.	11	3	4	1	1	1
9.	5	4	--	1	--	--
MEAN:	3.554	3.467	3.722	3.500	3.417	4.000
MEDIAN:	3.603	3.400	3.667	3.643	3.667	4.000
MODE:	4.000	3.000	3.000	4.000	4.000	4.000
STD. DEV.:	.909	1.060	.895	.855	.996	.632

NOTE: The following question applies to #'s 23-26 below. "To what extent do the following organizations within the Church provide information on world events of concern (e.g., Poland, El Salvadore, etc.)?"

23. The National Conference of Catholic Bishops

FREQUENCIES:	General Population	1-10%	11-20%	21-30%	31-40%	41-50%
1.	--	--	--	--	--	--
2.	4	1	--	2	--	--
3.	14	3	2	1	4	--
4.	28	7	7	5	3	5
5.	32	8	8	7	5	1
9.	1	--	1	--	--	--
MEAN:	4.128	4.158	4.353	4.133	4.083	4.167
MEDIAN:	4.250	4.286	4.429	4.400	4.167	4.100
MODE:	5.000	5.000	5.000	5.000	5.000	4.000
STD. DEV.:	.888	.898	.702	1.060	.900	.408

24. The National Federation of Priests' Councils

FREQUENCIES:	General Population	1-10%	11-20%	21-30%	31-40%	41-50%
1.	4	--	--	2	--	--
2.	22	2	6	4	5	2
3.	25	7	8	4	4	--
4.	18	6	2	3	2	4
5.	7	2	1	2	1	--
9.	3	2	1	--	--	--
MEAN:	3.026	3.471	2.882	2.933	2.917	3.333
MEDIAN:	2.980	3.429	2.813	2.875	2.750	3.350
MODE:	3.000	3.000	3.000	2.000	2.000	4.000
STD. DEV.:	1.058	.874	.857	1.280	.996	1.033

25. The Apostolic Delegation

FREQUENCIES:	General Population	1-10%	11-20%	21-30%	31-40%	41-50%
1.	23	3	9	4	2	1
2.	29	9	5	5	7	2
3.	18	5	4	2	2	2
4.	7	--	--	4	1	1
5.	--	--	--	--	--	--
9.	2	2	--	--	--	--
MEAN:	2.117	2.118	1.722	2.400	2.167	2.500
MEDIAN:	2.034	2.111	1.500	2.200	2.071	2.500
MODE:	2.000	2.000	1.000	2.000	2.000	2.000
STD. DEV.:	.946	.697	.826	1.183	.835	1.049

26. The State and/or U.S. Catholic Conference

FREQUENCIES:	General Population	1-10%	11-20%	21-30%	31-40%	41-50%
1.	--	--	--	--	--	--
2.	10	2	3	2	2	--
3.	22	3	6	4	4	2
4.	20	8	2	3	2	3
5.	25	6	6	5	4	1
9.	2	--	1	1	--	--
MEAN:	3.779	3.947	3.647	3.786	3.667	3.833
MEDIAN:	3.825	4.063	3.417	3.833	3.500	3.833
MODE:	5.000	4.000	3.000	5.000	3.000	4.000
STD. DEV.:	1.047	.970	1.169	1.122	1.155	.753

NOTE: The following question applies to #'s 27-30 below. "To what extent do the following organizations within the Church provide information on national events of concern (e.g., Human Rights, Abortion vs. Pro-life, etc.)?"

27. The National Conference of Catholic Bishops

FREQUENCIES:	General Population	1-10%	11-20%	21-30%	31-40%	41-50%
1.	--	--	--	--	--	--
2.	3	--	--	2	--	--
3.	8	3	2	1	1	--
4.	21	4	5	3	5	3
5.	47	12	11	9	6	3
9.	--	--	--	--	--	--
MEAN:	4.418	4.474	4.500	4.267	4.417	4.500
MEDIAN:	4.660	4.708	4.682	4.667	4.500	4.500
MODE:	5.000	5.000	5.000	5.000	5.000	4.000
STD. DEV.:	.826	.772	.707	1.100	.669	.548

28. The National Federation of Priests' Councils

FREQUENCIES:	General Population	1-10%	11-20%	21-30%	31-40%	41-50%
1.	4	--	--	2	--	--
2.	24	5	6	5	4	1
3.	27	6	10	5	3	2
4.	13	3	1	1	4	3
5.	9	3	1	2	1	--
9.	2	2	--	--	--	--
MEAN:	2.987	3.235	2.833	2.733	3.167	3.333
MEDIAN:	2.889	3.083	2.800	2.600	3.167	3.350
MODE:	3.000	3.000	3.000	2.000	2.000	4.000
STD. DEV.:	1.082	1.091	.786	1.223	1.130	.816

29. The Apostolic Delegation

FREQUENCIES:	General Population	1-10%	11-20%	21-30%	31-40%	41-50%
1.	26	3	10	4	3	2
2.	26	9	3	5	6	1
3.	17	5	5	3	--	3
4.	6	--	--	2	2	--
5.	2	--	--	1	1	--
9.	2	2	--	--	--	--
MEAN:	2.117	2.118	1.722	2.400	2.333	2.167
MEDIAN:	1.981	2.111	1.400	2.200	2.000	2.500
MODE:	1.000	2.000	1.000	2.000	2.000	3.000
STD. DEV.:	1.051	.967	.895	1.242	1.303	.983

30. The State and/or U.S. Catholic Conference

FREQUENCIES:	General Population	1-10%	11-20%	21-30%	31-40%	41-50%
1.	--	--	--	--	--	--
2.	6	2	--	1	2	--
3.	16	3	6	5	1	1
4.	22	5	5	3	4	3
5.	34	9	7	5	5	2
9.	1	--	--	1	--	--
MEAN:	4.077	4.105	4.056	3.857	4.000	4.167
MEDIAN:	4.273	4.400	4.100	3.833	4.250	4.167
MODE:	5.000	5.000	5.000	3.000	5.000	4.000
STD. DEV.:	.977	1.049	.873	1.027	1.128	.753

NOTE: The following question applies to #'s 31-34 below. "To what extent do
the following organizations within the Church provide information on
local events of concern?"

31. The National Conference of Catholic Bishops

FREQUENCIES:	General Population	1-10%	11-20%	21-30%	31-40%	41-50%
1.	19	3	8	3	1	1
2.	36	10	7	7	5	4
3.	14	3	2	4	3	--
4.	5	1	--	1	1	1
5.	4	1	1	--	2	--
9.	1	1	--	--	--	--
MEAN:	2.218	2.278	1.833	2.200	2.833	2.167
MEDIAN:	2.056	2.100	1.643	2.143	2.500	2.000
MODE:	2.000	2.000	1.000	2.000	2.000	2.000
STD. DEV.:	1.052	1.018	1.043	.862	1.267	.983

32. The National Federation of Priests' Councils

FREQUENCIES:	General Population	1-10%	11-20%	21-30%	31-40%	41-50%
1.	30	4	10	7	4	1
2.	33	12	6	5	4	5
3.	11	1	2	3	3	--
4.	2	--	--	--	--	--
5.	--	--	--	--	--	--
9.	3	2	--	--	1	--
MEAN:	1.803	1.824	1.556	1.733	1.909	1.833
MEDIAN:	1.742	1.875	1.400	1.600	1.875	1.900
MODE:	2.000	2.000	1.000	1.000	1.000	2.000
STD. DEV.:	.783	.529	.705	.799	.831	.408

33. The Apostolic Delegation

FREQUENCIES:	General Population	1-10%	11-20%	21-30%	31-40%	41-50%
1.	44	9	13	8	6	3
2.	19	6	4	2	4	2
3.	11	1	1	5	1	1
4.	1	--	--	--	--	--
5.	1	--	--	--	1	--
9.	3	3	--	--	--	--
MEAN:	1.632	1.500	1.333	1.800	1.833	1.667
MEDIAN:	1.364	1.389	1.192	1.438	1.500	1.500
MODE:	1.000	1.000	1.000	1.000	1.000	1.000
STD. DEV.:	.877	.632	.594	.941	1.193	.816

34. The State and/or U.S. Catholic Conference

FREQUENCIES:	General Population	1-10%	11-20%	21-30%	31-40%	41-50%
1.	8	3	3	2	---	--
2.	21	5	2	5	3	1
3.	17	4	5	5	1	--
4.	19	4	4	2	4	4
5.	13	2	4	1	4	1
9.	1	1	--	--	--	--
MEAN:	3.103	2.833	3.222	2.667	3.750	3.833
MEDIAN:	3.088	2.750	3.300	2.600	4.000	4.000
MODE:	2.000	2.000	3.000	2.000	4.000	4.000
STD. DEV.:	1.265	1.295	1.396	1.113	1.215	.983

35. To what extent is the current ordinary active in national bishop's organizations such as the NCCB?

FREQUENCIES:	General Population	1-10%	11-20%	21-30%	31-40%	41-50%
1.	2	1	1	--	--	--
2.	4	--	1	2	--	--
3.	14	3	3	2	1	2
4.	23	6	5	4	5	1
5.	36	9	8	7	6	3
9.	--	--	--	--	--	--
MEAN:	4.101	4.158	4.000	4.067	4.417	4.167
MEDIAN:	4.348	4.417	4.300	4.375	4.500	4.500
MODE:	5.000	5.000	5.000	5.000	5.000	5.000
STD. DEV.:	1.033	1.068	1.188	1.100	.669	.983

36. To what extent was the previous ordinary active in national bishop's organizations such as the NCCB?

FREQUENCIES:	General Population	1-10%	11-20%	21-30%	31-40%	41-50%
1.	4	--	1	1	--	--
2.	18	4	5	3	4	--
3.	27	6	9	3	4	3
4.	16	3	3	4	1	2
5.	8	3	--	2	2	1
9.	6	3	--	2	1	--
MEAN:	3.082	3.313	2.778	3.231	3.091	3.667
MEDIAN:	3.037	3.167	2.833	3.333	2.875	3.500
MODE:	3.000	3.000	3.000	4.000	2.000	3.000
STD. DEV.:	1.064	1.078	.808	1.235	1.136	.816

37. To what extent is the Church's hierarchy (e.g., the Apostolic Delegation, the Vatican) consulted by the diocese as it researches a problem and determines a course of action?

FREQUENCIES:	General Population	1-10%	11-20%	21-30%	31-40%	41-50%
1.	7	1	3	1	2	--
2.	29	8	7	7	2	1
3.	30	6	7	5	4	4
4.	12	3	1	2	4	1
5.	1	1	--	--	--	--
9.	--	--	--	--	--	--
MEAN:	2.633	2.737	2.333	2.533	2.833	3.000
MEDIAN:	2.617	2.583	2.357	2.429	3.000	3.000
MODE:	3.000	2.000	2.000	2.000	3.000	3.000
STD. DEV.:	.894	.991	.840	.834	1.115	.632

38. To what extent are other units of the Church (e.g., other dioceses) consulted by your diocese as it researches a problem and determines a course of action?

FREQUENCIES:	General Population	1-10%	11-20%	21-30%	31-40%	41-50%
1.	3	2	1	--	--	--
2.	12	1	3	1	3	--
3.	32	6	7	11	3	4
4.	27	8	5	3	6	1
5.	5	2	2	--	--	1
9.	--	--	--	--	--	--
MEAN:	3.241	3.368	3.222	3.133	3.250	3.500
MEDIAN:	3.266	3.563	3.214	3.091	3.500	3.250
MODE:	3.000	4.000	3.000	3.000	4.000	3.000
STD. DEV.:	.923	1.116	1.060	.516	.866	.837

39. To what extent is the current ordinary supportive of agents of the diocese (clergy, etc.) actively taking a position on issues of social concern?

FREQUENCIES:	General Population	1-10%	11-20%	21-30%	31-40%	41-50%
1.	--	--	--	--	--	--
2.	7	2	2	2	--	--
3.	13	2	1	3	4	1
4.	31	6	10	7	3	3
5.	28	9	5	3	5	2
9.	--	--	--	--	--	--
MEAN:	4.013	4.158	4.000	3.733	4.083	4.167
MEDIAN:	4.129	4.417	4.100	3.857	4.167	4.167
MODE:	4.000	5.000	4.000	4.000	5.000	4.000
STD. DEV.:	.940	1.015	.907	.961	.900	.753

40. To what extent was the <u>previous ordinary</u> supportive of agents of the diocese (clergy, etc.) actively taking a position on local issues of social concern?

FREQUENCIES:	General Population	1-10%	11-20%	21-30%	31-40%	41-50%
1.	2	--	--	1	--	--
2.	17	6	4	1	2	1
3.	25	4	9	6	4	1
4.	19	3	4	4	4	3
5.	10	3	1	1	1	1
9.	6	3	--	2	1	--
MEAN:	3.247	3.188	3.111	3.231	3.364	3.667
MEDIAN:	3.200	3.000	3.056	3.250	3.375	3.833
MODE:	3.000	2.000	3.000	3.000	3.000	4.000
STD. DEV.:	1.051	1.167	.832	1.013	.924	1.033

41. To what extent does the diocese work with or through <u>government agencies</u> to offer such things as community education programs on drug abuse, alcohol abuse, human equality, etc.?

FREQUENCIES:	General Population	1-10%	11-20%	21-30%	31-40%	41-50%
1.	2	--	--	1	--	1
2.	24	3	11	4	4	1
3.	22	6	4	6	3	1
4.	19	6	3	4	--	3
5.	12	4	--	--	5	--
9.	--	--	--	--	--	--
MEAN:	3.190	3.579	2.556	2.867	3.500	3.000
MEDIAN:	3.114	3.583	2.318	2.917	3.167	3.500
MODE:	2.000	3.000	2.000	3.000	5.000	4.000
STD. DEV.:	1.110	1.017	.784	.915	1.382	1.265

42. To what extent does the diocese work with or through <u>business organizations</u> to offer such things as community education programs on drug abuse, human equality, etc.?

FREQUENCIES:	General Population	1-10%	11-20%	21-30%	31-40%	41-50%
1.	14	4	5	3	1	--
2.	30	6	10	5	5	2
3.	23	4	3	7	4	2
4.	10	4	--	--	2	2
5.	2	1	--	--	--	--
9.	--	--	--	--	--	--
MEAN:	2.443	2.579	1.889	2.267	2.583	3.000
MEDIAN:	2.350	2.417	1.900	2.400	2.500	3.000
MODE:	2.000	2.000	2.000	3.000	2.000	2.000
STD. DEV.:	1.010	1.216	.676	.799	.900	.894

43. To what extent is the <u>current ordinary</u> active in the local community (e.g., on community boards and commissions, active in various areas of community concern)?

FREQUENCIES:	General Population	1-10%	11-20%	21-30%	31-40%	41-50%
1.	3	2	--	1	--	--
2.	20	3	9	4	1	--
3.	25	4	5	5	7	2
4.	20	6	2	4	2	3
5.	11	4	2	1	2	1
9.	--	--	--	--	--	--
MEAN:	3.203	3.368	2.833	3.000	3.417	3.833
MEDIAN:	3.160	3.583	2.500	3.000	3.214	3.833
MODE:	3.000	4.000	2.000	3.000	3.000	4.000
STD. DEV.:	1.091	1.300	1.043	1.069	.900	.753

44. To what extent was the <u>previous ordinary</u> active in the local community (e.g., on community boards and commissions, active in various areas of community concern)?

FREQUENCIES:	General Population	1-10%	11-20%	21-30%	31-40%	41-50%
1.	6	--	2	1	1	1
2.	30	7	10	4	5	1
3.	20	4	4	6	3	2
4.	13	3	2	1	2	2
5.	4	2	--	1	--	--
9.	6	3	--	2	1	--
MEAN:	2.712	3.000	2.333	2.769	2.545	2.833
MEDIAN:	2.525	2.750	2.200	2.750	2.400	3.000
MODE:	2.000	2.000	2.000	3.000	2.000	3.000
STD. DEV.:	1.034	1.095	.840	1.013	.934	1.169

45. To what extent does the <u>current ordinary</u> travel to visit individual parishes in the diocese?

FREQUENCIES:	General Population	1-10%	11-20%	21-30%	31-40%	41-50%
1.	--	--	--	--	--	--
2.	3	1	--	1	--	--
3.	7	1	3	--	2	--
4.	17	3	2	4	2	2
5.	52	14	13	10	8	4
9.	--	--	--	--	--	--
MEAN:	4.494	4.579	4.556	4.533	4.500	4.667
MEDIAN:	4.740	4.821	4.808	4.750	4.750	4.750
MODE:	5.000	5.000	5.000	5.000	5.000	5.000
STD. DEV.:	.815	.838	.784	.834	.798	.516

46. To what extent did the previous ordinary travel to visit individual parishes in the diocese?

FREQUENCIES:	General Population	1-10%	11-20%	21-30%	31-40%	41-50%
1.	1	--	1	--	--	--
2.	7	11	3	1	1	--
3.	16	3	4	1	3	2
4.	30	4	5	8	4	4
5.	19	8	5	3	3	--
9.	6	3	--	2	1	--
MEAN:	3.808	4.188	3.556	4.000	3.818	3.667
MEDIAN:	3.917	4.500	3.700	4.063	3.875	3.750
MODE:	4.000	5.000	4.000	4.000	4.000	4.000
STD. DEV.:	.981	.981	1.247	.816	.982	.516

47. To what extent do individual parishes have a voice in the major decisions of the diocese?

FREQUENCIES:	General Population	1-10%	11-20%	21-30%	31-40%	41-50%
1.	7	2	2	--	2	--
2.	17	3	3	4	4	--
3.	29	4	4	9	5	5
4.	21	8	7	2	1	--
5.	5	2	2	--	--	1
9.	--	--	--	--	--	--
MEAN:	3.000	3.263	3.222	2.867	2.417	3.333
MEDIAN:	3.034	3.563	3.500	2.889	2.500	3.200
MODE:	3.000	4.000	4.000	3.000	3.000	3.000
STD. DEV.:	1.050	1.195	1.215	.640	.900	.816

48. To what extent are the parishes of the diocese in a state of harmony on local issues facing the diocese?

FREQUENCIES:	General Population	1-10%	11-20%	21-30%	31-40%	41-50%
1.	1	1	--	--	--	--
2.	6	1	2	2	1	--
3.	37	7	9	7	8	1
4.	29	10	3	6	3	4
5.	5	--	3	--	--	1
9.	1	--	1	--	--	--
MEAN:	3.397	3.368	3.412	3.267	3.167	4.000
MEDIAN:	3.365	3.550	3.222	3.286	3.125	4.000
MODE:	3.000	4.000	3.000	3.000	3.000	4.000
STD. DEV.:	.779	.831	.939	.704	.577	.632

49. To what extent are the priests in the diocese aware of the existence of the Priests' Senate?

FREQUENCIES:	General Population	1-10%	11-20%	21-30%	31-40%	41-50%
1.	--	--	--	--	--	--
2.	2	2	--	--	--	--
3.	3	--	--	--	2	--
4.	17	5	2	4	3	1
5.	54	11	16	11	7	5
9.	3	1	--	--	--	--
MEAN:	4.618	4.389	4.889	4.733	4.417	4.833
MEDIAN:	4.796	4.682	4.938	4.818	4.643	4.900
MODE:	5.000	5.000	5.000	5.000	5.000	5.000
STD. DEV.:	.692	.979	.323	.458	.793	.408

50. To what extent have the priests in the diocese been able to use the Priests' Senate to express their concerns?

FREQUENCIES:	General Population	1-10%	11-20%	21-30%	31-40%	41-50%
1.	1	--	--	--	1	--
2.	2	2	--	--	--	--
3.	13	5	1	1	4	--
4.	28	4	6	7	4	3
5.	33	7	11	7	3	3
9.	2	1	--	--	--	--
MEAN:	4.169	3.889	4.556	4.400	3.667	4.500
MEDIAN:	4.304	4.000	4.682	4.429	3.750	4.500
MODE:	5.000	5.000	5.000	4.000	3.000	4.000
STD. DEV.:	.894	1.079	.616	.632	1.155	.548

51. To what extent does the diocese as a whole join forces with other major faiths in the community (e.g., Lutheran, Methodist, Presbyterian, Jewish, etc.) in addressing issues of local concern?

FREQUENCIES:	General Population	1-10%	11-20%	21-30%	31-40%	41-50%
1.	2	--	--	1	1	--
2.	9	--	6	2	1	--
3.	26	3	8	4	5	3
4.	30	10	2	6	4	3
5.	12	6	2	2	1	--
9.	--	--	--	--	--	--
MEAN:	3.519	4.158	3.000	3.400	3.250	3.500
MEDIAN:	3.583	4.150	2.875	3.583	3.300	3.500
MODE:	4.000	4.000	3.000	4.000	3.000	3.000
STD. DEV.:	.972	.688	.970	1.121	1.055	.548

52. What percentage of diocesan clergy are active in local ministerial organizations (local groups of ministers from various denominations who meet to address issues of concern in their area)?

           1. 0-20%   4. 61-80%
           2. 21-40%   5. 81-100%
           3. 41-60%   9. No response

FREQUENCIES:	General Population	1-10%	11-20%	21-30%	31-40%	41-50%
1.	22	5	7	5	3	1
2.	28	6	6	5	3	2
3.	24	6	4	5	5	3
4.	5	2	1	--	1	--
5.	--	--	--	--	--	--
9.	--	--	--	--	--	--
MEAN:	2.152	2.263	1.944	2.000	2.333	2.333
MEDIAN:	2.125	2.250	2.833	2.000	2.500	2.500
MODE:	2.000	2.000	1.000	1.000	3.000	3.000
STD. DEV.:	.907	.991	.938	.845	.985	.816

53. Is the diocese a member of any community-wide ecumenical organizations (such as a council of churches) on a long-term basis?

           1. Yes
           2. No
           9. No response

FREQUENCIES:	General Population	1-10%	11-20%	21-30%	31-40%	41-50%
1.	55	16	13	8	7	3
2.	21	2	4	6	5	3
9.	3	1	1	1	--	--
MEAN:	1.325	1.111	1.444	1.429	1.417	1.500
MEDIAN:	1.200	1.063	1.192	1.375	1.357	1.500
MODE:	1.000	1.000	1.000	1.000	1.000	1.000
STD. DEV.:	.616	.323	.982	.514	.515	.548

54. What portion of the parishes of the diocese have parish councils?

           1. 0-20%   4. 61-80%
           2. 21-40%   5. 81-100%
           3. 41-60%   9. No response

FREQUENCIES:	General Population	1-10%	11-20%	21-30%	31-40%	41-50%
1.	2	--	2	--	--	--
2.	5	2	--	2	--	--
3.	11	1	3	4	--	1
4.	18	3	4	4	5	2
5.	42	13	9	5	7	2
9.	1	--	--	--	--	1
MEAN:	4.228	4.421	4.000	3.800	4.583	4.667
MEDIAN:	4.583	4.769	4.500	3.875	4.643	4.500
MODE:	5.000	5.000	5.000	5.000	5.000	4.000
STD. DEV.:	1.109	1.017	1.328	1.082	.515	1.366

55. Is there currently a working pastoral council in the diocese?

       1. Yes
       2. No
       9. No response

FREQUENCIES:	General Population	1-10%	11-20%	21-30%	31-40%	41-50%
1.	44	8	12	9	8	3
2.	34	11	6	6	4	2
9.	1	--	--	--	--	1
MEAN:	1.481	1.579	1.333	1.400	1.333	2.000
MEDIAN:	1.398	1.636	1.250	1.333	1.250	1.500
MODE:	1.000	2.000	1.000	1.000	1.000	1.000
STD. DEV.:	.638	.507	.485	.507	.492	1.549

NOTE: The following question applies to #'s 56-60 below. "To what extent would the following qualities be important in a lay person serving on a pastoral council?"

56. Active in parish organizations

FREQUENCIES:	General Population	1-10%	11-20%	21-30%	31-40%	41-50%
1.	--	--	--	--	--	--
2.	3	1	1	1	--	--
3.	15	4	3	1	4	--
4.	32	8	8	9	2	3
5.	27	5	6	4	6	3
9.	2	1	--	--	--	--
MEAN:	4.078	3.944	4.056	4.067	4.167	4.500
MEDIAN:	4.141	4.000	4.125	4.111	4.500	4.500
MODE:	4.000	4.000	4.000	4.000	5.000	4.000
STD. DEV.:	.839	.873	.873	.799	.937	.548

57. Active in non-church community organizations

FREQUENCIES:	General Population	1-10%	11-20%	21-30%	31-40%	41-50%
1.	2	1	1	--	--	--
2.	26	4	8	6	4	1
3.	29	10	6	5	4	--
4.	13	2	1	3	3	3
5.	6	1	2	--	1	2
9.	3	1	--	1	--	--
MEAN:	2.934	2.889	2.722	2.786	3.083	4.000
MEDIAN:	2.845	2.900	2.500	2.700	3.000	4.167
MODE:	3.000	3.000	2.000	2.000	2.000	4.000
STD. DEV.:	.971	.900	1.074	.802	.996	1.095

58. Have a knowledge of the organization of the diocese

FREQUENCIES:	General Population	1-10%	11-20%	21-30%	31-40%	41-50%
1.	1	1	--	--	--	--
2.	11	1	3	2	3	2
3.	24	7	4	5	5	--
4.	29	5	8	7	2	2
5.	11	3	3	1	2	2
9.	3	2	--	--	--	--
MEAN:	3.500	3.471	3.611	3.467	3.250	3.667
MEDIAN:	3.569	3.429	3.750	3.571	3.100	4.000
MODE:	4.000	3.000	4.000	4.000	3.000	2.000
STD. DEV.:	.959	1.068	.979	.834	1.055	1.366

59. Have experience in other diocesan-wide committees and activities

FREQUENCIES:	General Population	1-10%	11-20%	21-30%	31-40%	41-50%
1.	1	1	--	--	--	--
2.	10	3	2	4	1	--
3.	30	8	8	5	4	--
4.	27	5	5	5	5	4
5.	8	1	2	1	2	2
9.	3	1	1	--	--	--
MEAN:	3.408	3.111	3.412	3.200	3.667	4.333
MEDIAN:	3.400	3.125	3.313	3.200	3.700	4.250
MODE:	3.000	3.000	3.000	3.000	4.000	4.000
STD. DEV.:	.897	.963	.870	.941	.888	.516

60. Be able to represent specific groups and/or current concerns of community

FREQUENCIES:	General Population	1-10%	11-20%	21-30%	31-40%	41-50%
1.	2	--	1	1	--	--
2.	5	1	--	1	2	1
3.	22	6	5	5	3	1
4.	28	5	6	7	4	2
5.	13	2	5	--	3	2
9.	9	5	1	1	--	--
MEAN:	3.643	3.571	3.824	3.286	3.667	3.833
MEDIAN:	3.714	3.500	3.917	3.500	3.750	4.000
MODE:	4.000	3.000	4.000	4.000	4.000	4.000
STD. DEV.:	.964	.852	1.074	.914	1.073	1.169

61. To what extent does the present ordinary support the existence (or future formation) of a pastoral council?

FREQUENCIES:	General Population	1-10%	11-20%	21-30%	31-40%	41-50%
1.	1	1	--	--	--	--
2.	4	--	1	1	1	1
3.	16	6	2	2	2	2
4.	13	1	2	4	3	--
5.	43	10	13	8	6	3
9.	2	1	--	--	--	--
MEAN:	4.208	4.056	4.500	4.267	4.167	3.833
MEDIAN:	4.605	4.600	4.808	4.563	4.500	3.500
MODE:	5.000	5.000	5.000	5.000	5.000	5.000
STD. DEV.:	1.030	1.211	.924	.961	1.030	1.329

NOTE: The following question applies to #'s 62-69 below. "To what extent would the following characteristics be required of a bishop to serve successfully as ordinary of your diocese?"

62. Be a biblical scholar

FREQUENCIES:	General Population	1-10%	11-20%	21-30%	31-40%	41-50%
1.	9	1	4	1	3	--
2.	25	9	4	6	2	3
3.	34	7	7	5	5	3
4.	5	--	2	1	2	--
5.	4	1	1	2	--	--
9.	2	1	--	--	--	--
MEAN:	2.610	2.500	2.556	2.800	2.500	2.500
MEDIAN:	2.632	2.389	2.643	2.600	2.700	2.500
MODE:	3.000	2.000	3.000	2.000	3.000	2.000
STD. DEV.:	.962	.857	1.149	1.146	1.087	.548

63. Be a temporal scholar

FREQUENCIES:	General Population	1-10%	11-20%	21-30%	31-40%	41-50%
1.	13	1	4	2	4	--
2.	19	7	3	5	--	3
3.	36	9	9	6	6	2
4.	6	--	1	2	1	1
5.	3	1	1	--	1	--
9.	2	1	--	--	--	--
MEAN:	2.571	2.611	2.556	2.533	2.583	2.667
MEDIAN:	2.681	2.611	2.722	2.583	2.833	2.500
MODE:	3.000	3.000	3.000	3.000	3.000	2.000
STD. DEV.:	.992	.850	1.097	.915	1.311	.816

64. Personal charm or charisma

FREQUENCIES:	General Population	1-10%	11-20%	21-30%	31-40%	41-50%
1.	1	--	1	--	--	--
2.	6	--	1	3	1	--
3.	27	5	7	5	6	2
4.	30	8	7	5	4	2
5.	13	5	2	2	1	2
9.	2	1	--	--	--	--
MEAN:	3.623	4.000	3.444	3.400	3.417	4.000
MEDIAN:	3.650	4.000	3.500	3.400	3.333	4.000
MODE:	4.000	4.000	3.000	3.000	3.000	3.000
STD. DEV.:	.904	.767	.984	.986	.793	.894

65. Ability to empathize with individual problems

FREQUENCIES:	General Population	1-10%	11-20%	21-30%	31-40%	41-50%
1.	--	--	--	--	--	--
2.	1	--	--	1	--	--
3.	12	--	6	2	2	1
4.	41	10	7	8	6	5
5.	22	7	5	4	4	--
9.	3	2	--	--	--	--
MEAN:	4.105	4.412	3.944	4.000	4.167	3.833
MEDIAN:	4.110	4.350	3.929	4.063	4.167	3.900
MODE:	4.000	4.000	4.000	4.000	4.000	4.000
STD. DEV.:	.704	.507	.802	.845	.718	.408

66. Be "an organizer"

FREQUENCIES:	General Population	1-10%	11-20%	21-30%	31-40%	41-50%
1.	1	--	--	1	--	--
2.	2	1	1	--	--	--
3.	26	4	2	7	6	4
4.	35	9	13	3	4	2
5.	13	4	2	4	2	--
9.	2	1	--	--	--	--
MEAN:	3.740	3.889	3.889	3.600	3.667	3.333
MEDIAN:	3.771	3.944	3.962	3.429	3.500	3.250
MODE:	4.000	4.000	4.000	3.000	3.000	3.000
STD. DEV.:	.818	.832	.676	1.121	.778	.516

67. Be proficient at establishing contacts in the local community

FREQUENCIES:	General Population	1-10%	11-20%	21-30%	31-40%	41-50%
1.	--	--	--	--	--	--
2.	8	1	1	3	2	1
3.	25	5	7	3	5	2
4.	34	10	9	5	3	3
5.	10	2	1	4	2	--
9.	2	1	--	--	--	--
MEAN:	3.597	3.722	3.556	3.667	3.417	3.333
MEDIAN:	3.662	3.800	3.611	3.800	3.300	3.500
MODE:	4.000	4.000	4.000	4.000	3.000	4.000
STD. DEV.:	.847	.752	.705	1.113	.996	.816

68. Already have contacts in the local community

FREQUENCIES:	General Population	1-10%	11-20%	21-30%	31-40%	41-50%
1.	18	3	5	4	3	2
2.	28	7	6	7	4	1
3.	12	4	4	1	1	1
4.	13	3	2	2	2	1
5.	5	--	1	1	2	1
9.	3	2	--	--	--	--
MEAN:	2.461	2.412	2.333	2.267	2.667	2.667
MEDIAN:	2.214	2.286	2.167	2.000	2.250	2.500
MODE:	2.000	2.000	2.000	2.000	2.000	1.000
STD. DEV.:	1.216	1.004	1.188	1.223	1.497	1.633

69. Sensitivity to the concerns of specific groups in the diocese

FREQUENCIES:	General Population	1-10%	11-20%	21-30%	31-40%	41-50%
1.	--	--	--	--	--	--
2.	2	--	1	--	1	--
3.	15	3	4	2	1	3
4.	32	5	8	10	3	2
5.	26	9	5	3	7	1
9.	4	2	--	--	--	--
MEAN:	4.093	4.353	3.944	4.067	4.333	3.667
MEDIAN:	4.141	4.556	4.000	4.050	4.643	3.500
MODE:	4.000	5.000	4.000	4.000	5.000	3.000
STD. DEV.:	.808	.786	.873	.594	.985	.816

70. What portion of the total population in the area of your diocese is Catholic?

FREQUENCIES: General Population

0-10%: 19	61-70%: 1
11-20%: 18	71-80%: 1
21-30%: 15	81-90%: 0
31-40%: 12	91-100%: 1
41-50%: 6	
51-60%: 6	TOTAL: 79 respondents

71. What percentage of the diocese's operating income is obtained from the parishes in the diocese through the general collection?

1. 0-20%   4. 61-80%
2. 21-40%   5. 81-100%
3. 41-60%   9. No response

FREQUENCIES:	General Population	1-10%	11-20%	21-30%	31-40%	41-50%
1.	14	3	3	3	2	1
2.	12	4	2	1	2	1
3.	10	5	1	1	2	1
4.	21	3	4	7	3	2
5.	20	4	6	3	3	1
9.	2	--	2	--	--	--
MEAN:	3.273	3.053	3.500	3.400	3.250	3.167
MEDIAN:	3.619	3.000	4.000	3.857	3.500	3.500
MODE:	4.000	3.000	5.000	4.000	4.000	4.000
STD. DEV.:	1.466	1.393	1.592	1.454	1.485	1.472

72. What percentage of the diocese's operating income is obtained from sources outside the diocese such as the gifts of organizations?

1. 0-20%   4. 61-80%
2. 21-40%   5. 81-100%
3. 41-60%   9. No response

FREQUENCIES:	General Population	1-10%	11-20%	21-30%	31-40%	41-50%
1.	70	16	17	12	11	6
2.	8	3	1	2	1	--
3.	1	--	--	1	--	--
4.	--	--	--	--	--	--
5.	--	--	--	--	--	--
9.	--	--	--	--	--	--
MEAN:	1.127	1.158	1.056	1.267	1.083	1.000
MEDIAN:	1.064	1.094	1.029	1.125	1.045	1.000
MODE:	1.000	1.000	1.000	1.000	1.000	1.000
STD. DEV.:	.371	.375	.236	.594	.289	0

73. What percentage of the diocese's operating income is obtained from rents on lands and properties owned by the diocese?

```
        1.  0-20%     4.  61-80%
        2.  21-40%    5.  81-100%
        3.  41-60%    9.  No response
```

FREQUENCIES:	General Population	1-10%	11-20%	21-30%	31-40%	41-50%
1.	78	18	18	15	12	6
2.	1	1	--	--	--	--
3.	--	--	--	--	--	--
4.	--	--	--	--	--	--
5.	--	--	--	--	--	--
9.	--	--	--	--	--	--
MEAN:	1.013	1.053	1.000	1.000	1.000	1.000
MEDIAN:	1.006	1.028	1.000	1.000	1.000	1.000
MODE:	1.000	1.000	1.000	1.000	1.000	1.000
STD. DEV.:	.113	.229	0	0	0	0

74. What percentage of the diocese's income is obtained from returns on stocks and similar investments?

```
        1.  0-20%     4.  61-80%
        2.  21-40%    5.  81-100%
        3.  41-60%    9.  No response
```

FREQUENCIES:	General Population	1-10%	11-20%	21-30%	31-40%	41-50%
1.	64	14	13	14	11	6
2.	10	3	3	1	1	--
3.	3	1	1	--	--	--
4.	1	--	1	--	--	--
5.	--	--	--	--	--	--
9.	1	1	--	--	--	--
MEAN:	1.244	1.278	1.444	1.067	1.083	1.000
MEDIAN:	1.109	1.143	1.192	1.036	1.045	1.000
MODE:	1.000	1.000	1.000	1.000	1.000	1.000
STD. DEV.:	.585	.575	.856	.258	.289	0

NOTE: The following question applies to #'s 75-81 below. "To what extent does the diocese invest excess funds (when it has them) in:"

75. A bank savings account

FREQUENCIES:	General Population	1-10%	11-20%	21-30%	31-40%	41-50%
1.	18	6	6	3	1	1
2.	18	7	2	2	4	1
3.	10	1	2	2	2	1
4.	12	2	2	4	1	2
5.	15	2	6	2	2	1
9.	6	1	--	2	2	--
MEAN:	2.836	2.278	3.000	3.000	2.900	3.167
MEDIAN:	2.550	1.929	3.000	3.250	2.500	3.507
MODE:	1.000	2.000	1.000	4.000	2.000	4.000
STD. DEV.:	1.491	1.364	1.749	1.472	1.370	1.472

76. Bonds

FREQUENCIES:	General Population	1-10%	11-20%	21-30%	31-40%	41-50%
1.	17	6	5	2	1	1
2.	24	6	6	4	2	1
3.	13	3	2	3	2	3
4.	14	1	4	4	3	1
5.	5	2	1	--	2	--
9.	6	1	--	2	2	--
MEAN:	2.534	2.278	2.444	2.692	3.300	2.667
MEDIAN:	2.313	2.000	2.167	2.667	3.500	2.833
MODE:	2.000	1.000	2.000	2.000	4.000	3.000
STD. DEV.:	1.237	1.320	1.294	1.109	1.337	1.033

77. Stocks

FREQUENCIES:	General Population	1-10%	11-20%	21-30%	31-40%	41-50%
1.	19	5	6	2	1	2
2.	24	6	4	5	4	2
3.	14	2	3	4	2	2
4.	9	3	1	2	2	--
5.	7	2	3	--	2	--
9.	6	1	1	2	1	--
MEAN:	2.466	2.500	2.471	2.462	3.000	2.000
MEDIAN:	2.229	2.167	2.125	2.400	2.750	2.000
MODE:	2.000	2.000	1.000	2.000	2.000	1.000
STD. DEV.:	1.270	1.383	1.505	.967	1.342	.894

78. Property

FREQUENCIES:	General Population	1-10%	11-20%	21-30%	31-40%	41-50%
1.	27	7	10	1	4	3
2.	26	4	4	6	4	3
3.	13	6	2	4	--	--
4.	4	--	1	2	1	--
5.	2	1	1	--	--	--
9.	7	1	--	2	3	--
MEAN:	2.000	2.111	1.833	2.538	1.778	1.500
MEDIAN:	1.846	2.000	1.400	2.417	1.625	1.500
MODE:	1.000	1.000	1.000	2.000	1.000	1.000
STD. DEV.:	1.021	1.132	1.200	.877	.972	.548

79. Lend to individual parishes

FREQUENCIES:	General Population	1-10%	11-20%	21-30%	31-40%	41-50%
1.	11	4	4	1	1	1
2.	11	--	3	3	4	--
3.	14	5	2	2	2	2
4.	17	5	2	4	1	1
5.	20	4	6	4	2	2
9.	6	1	1	1	2	--
MEAN:	3.329	3.278	3.176	3.500	2.900	3.500
MEDIAN:	3.529	3.500	3.250	2.750	2.500	3.500
MODE:	5.000	3.000	5.000	4.000	2.000	3.000
STD. DEV.:	1.415	1.447	1.667	1.345	1.370	1.517

80. Lend to other dioceses

FREQUENCIES:	General Population	1-10%	11-20%	21-30%	31-40%	41-50%
1.	57	15	13	8	9	5
2.	13	3	3	4	1	1
3.	--	--	--	--	--	--
4.	1	--	--	1	--	--
5.	--	--	--	--	--	--
9.	8	1	2	2	2	--
MEAN:	1.225	1.167	1.188	1.538	1.100	1.167
MEDIAN:	1.123	1.100	1.115	1.313	1.056	1.100
MODE:	1.000	1.000	1.000	1.000	1.000	1.000
STD. DEV.:	.513	.383	.403	.877	.316	.408

81. Lend to Church hierarchy

FREQUENCIES:	General Population	1-10%	11-20%	21-30%	31-40%	41-50%
1.	68	17	17	11	10	6
2.	5	1	1	2	--	--
3.	--	--	--	--	--	--
4.	--	--	--	--	--	--
5.	--	--	--	--	--	--
9.	6	1	--	2	2	--
MEAN:	1.068	1.056	1.056	1.154	1.000	1.000
MEDIAN:	1.037	1.029	1.029	1.091	1.000	1.000
MODE:	1.000	1.000	1.000	1.000	1.000	1.000
STD. DEV.:	.254	.236	.236	.376	0	0

82. What percentage of Catholic school children in your diocese are enrolled in Catholic primary schools (K-8)?

    1. 0-20%   4. 61-80%
    2. 20-40%   5. 81-100%
    3. 41-60%   9. No response

FREQUENCIES:	General Population	1-10%	11-20%	21-30%	31-40%	41-50%
1.	25	5	8	4	3	1
2.	36	9	5	8	7	2
3.	14	4	5	2	1	2
4.	2	1	--	--	--	1
5.	--	--	--	--	--	--
9.	2	--	--	1	1	--
MEAN:	1.909	2.053	1.833	1.857	1.818	2.500
MEDIAN:	1.875	2.000	1.700	1.875	1.857	2.500
MODE:	2.000	2.000	1.000	2.000	2.000	2.000
STD. DEV.:	.781	.848	.857	.663	.603	1.049

83. What percentage of the <u>public</u> board of education in your community is made up of Catholics?

    1. 0-20%   4. 61-80%
    2. 21-40%   5. 81-100%
    3. 41-60%   9. No response

FREQUENCIES:	General Population	1-10%	11-20%	21-30%	21-40%	41-50%
1.	51	17	16	11	3	1
2.	13	1	1	1	7	2
3.	7	1	--	1	--	3
4.	2	--	--	--	1	--
5.	--	--	--	--	--	--
9.	6	--	1	2	1	--
MEAN:	1.452	1.158	1.059	1.231	1.909	2.333
MEDIAN:	1.216	1.059	1.031	1.091	1.857	2.500
MODE:	1.000	1.000	1.000	1.000	2.000	3.000
STD. DEV.:	.782	.501	.243	.599	.831	.816

84. Does your diocese have a diocesan-wide Board of Catholic Education?

    1. Yes -- over 50% are lay people
    2. Yes -- about 50% are lay people and 50% are clergy/religious
    3. Yes -- over 50% are clergy/religious
    4. No -- there is no diocesan-wide Board of Catholic Education
    9. No response

FREQUENCIES:	General Population	1-10%	11-20%	21-30%	31-40%	41-50%
1.	49	11	11	12	7	3
2.	11	2	3	1	1	3
3.	2	1	1	--	--	--
4.	17	5	3	2	4	--
9.	--	--	--	--	--	--
MEAN:	1.835	2.000	1.778	1.467	2.083	1.500
MEDIAN:	1.306	1.364	1.318	1.125	1.357	1.500
MODE:	1.000	1.000	1.000	1.000	1.000	1.000
STD. DEV.:	1.224	1.333	1.166	1.060	1.443	.548

NOTE: The following question applies to #'s 85-90 below. "To what extent would
the following qualities be important in a lay person serving on the
diocesan Board of Catholic Education?"

85. Active in parish organizations

FREQUENCIES:	General Population	1-10%	11-20%	21-30%	31-40%	41-50%
1.	1	--	1	--	--	--
2.	8	3	1	4	--	--
3.	23	5	6	3	5	1
4.	20	3	3	5	2	4
5.	12	4	4	1	2	1
9.	15	4	3	2	3	--
MEAN:	3.531	3.533	3.533	3.231	3.667	4.000
MEDIAN:	3.500	3.400	3.417	3.333	3.400	4.000
MODE:	3.000	3.000	3.000	4.000	3.000	4.000
STD. DEV.:	.992	1.125	1.187	1.013	.866	.632

86. Active in non-Church community organizations

FREQUENCIES:	General Population	1-10%	11-20%	21-30%	31-40%	41-50%
1.	6	1	2	1	2	--
2.	24	6	6	4	3	2
3.	24	6	5	7	3	1
4.	9	2	1	1	1	3
5.	1	--	1	--	--	--
9.	15	4	3	2	3	--
MEAN:	2.609	2.600	2.533	2.615	2.333	3.167
MEDIAN:	2.583	2.583	2.417	2.714	2.333	3.500
MODE:	2.000	2.000	2.000	3.000	2.000	4.000
STD. DEV.:	.902	.828	1.060	.768	1.000	.983

87. Have experience in other diocesan-wide committees and activities

FREQUENCIES:	General Population	1-10%	11-20%	21-30%	31-40%	41-50%
1.	1	--	--	--	1	--
2.	14	4	3	4	2	--
3.	29	5	11	6	2	1
4.	15	5	--	3	1	5
5.	5	1	1	--	3	--
9.	15	4	3	2	3	--
MEAN:	3.141	3.200	2.933	2.923	3.333	3.833
MEDIAN:	3.086	3.200	2.909	2.917	3.250	3.900
MODE:	3.000	3.000	3.000	3.000	5.000	4.000
STD. DEV.:	.906	.941	.704	.760	1.500	.408

88. Are affiliated with other educators in the community

FREQUENCIES:	General Population	1-10%	11-20%	21-30%	31-40%	41-50%
1.	1	--	1	--	--	--
2.	7	3	1	1	2	--
3.	26	7	6	6	4	1
4.	25	3	0	6	3	4
5.	4	2	1	--	--	--
9.	16	4	3	2	3	1
MEAN:	3.381	3.267	3.333	3.385	3.111	3.800
MEDIAN:	3.404	3.143	3.417	3.417	3.125	3.875
MODE:	3.000	3.000	3.000	3.000	3.000	4.000
STD. DEV.:	.831	.961	.976	.650	.782	.447

89. Are affiliated with important groups in the community

FREQUENCIES:	General Population	1-10%	11-20%	21-30%	31-40%	41-50%
1.	3	--	3	--	--	--
2.	20	4	6	4	2	2
3.	26	6	5	7	4	1
4.	14	4	1	2	3	3
5.	1	1	--	--	--	--
9.	15	4	3	2	3	--
MEAN:	2.844	3.133	2.267	2.846	3.111	3.167
MEDIAN:	3.846	3.083	2.250	2.857	3.125	3.500
MODE:	3.000	3.000	2.000	3.000	3.000	4.000
STD. DEV.:	.877	.915	.884	.689	.782	.983

90. Have knowledge and/or experience in the field of education

FREQUENCIES:	General Population	1-10%	11-20%	21-30%	31-40%	41-50%
1.	--	--	--	--	--	--
2.	3	--	--	1	1	1
3.	14	4	2	3	2	1
4.	30	5	9	5	4	4
5.	17	6	4	4	2	--
9.	15	4	3	2	3	--
MEAN:	3.953	4.133	4.133	3.923	3.778	3.500
MEDIAN:	4.000	4.200	4.111	4.000	3.875	3.750
MODE:	4.000	5.000	4.000	4.000	4.000	4.000
STD. DEV.:	.825	.834	.640	.954	.972	.837

91. To what extent are the expenses of the diocesan schools covered by tuition?

1.	0-20%	4.	61-80%
2.	21-40%	5.	81-100%
3.	41-60%	9.	No response

FREQUENCIES:	General Population	1-10%	11-20%	21-30%	31-40%	41-50%
1.	3	--	1	--	1	--
2.	18	3	3	3	5	2
3.	23	9	6	7	--	--
4.	17	4	5	2	3	2
5.	4	--	--	--	1	1
9.	14	3	3	3	2	1

MEAN:	3.015	3.063	3.000	2.917	2.800	3.400
MEDIAN:	3.000	3.056	3.083	2.929	2.300	3.750
MODE:	3.000	3.000	3.000	3.000	2.000	2.000
STD. DEV.:	.992	.834	.926	.669	1.317	1.342

92. To what extent are the expenses of the diocesan schools covered by contribu-tions directly from individual parishes?

1.	0-20%	4.	61-80%
2.	2 -40%	5.	81-100%
3.	41-60%	9.	No response

FREQUENCIES:	General Population	1-10%	11-20%	21-30%	31-40%	41-50%
1.	16	3	3	--	4	3
2.	24	7	6	7	2	1
3.	20	5	4	6	2	1
4.	3	1	--	--	1	--
5.	3	--	2	--	1	--
9.	13	3	3	2	2	1

MEAN:	2.288	2.250	2.467	2.462	2.300	1.600
MEDIAN:	2.208	2.214	2.250	2.429	2.000	1.333
MODE:	2.000	2.000	2.000	2.000	1.000	1.000
STD. DEV.:	1.034	.856	1.246	.519	1.418	.894

93. To what extent are the expenses of the diocesan schools covered by funds allocated by the diocese?

1.	0-20%	4.	61-80%
22.	21-40%	5.	81-100%
3.	41-60%	9.	No response

FREQUENCIES:	General Population	1-10%	11-20%	21-30%	31-40%	41-50%
1.	57	14	14	11	8	4
2.	7	2	1	--	2	2
3.	1	--	--	1	--	--
4.	1	--	--	--	--	--
5.	--	--	--	--	--	--
9.	13	3	3	3	2	--

MEAN:	1.182	1.125	1.067	1.167	1.200	1.333
MEDIAN:	1.079	1.071	1.036	1.091	1.125	1.250
MODE:	1.000	1.000	1.000	1.000	1.000	1.000
STD. DEV.:	.524	.342	.258	.577	.422	.516

94. Does the diocese have a board of directors of Catholic Social Services (or of Catholic Charities)?

    1. Yes -- over 50% are lay people
    2. Yes -- about 50% are lay people and 50% are clergy/religious
    3. Yes -- over 50% are clergy/religious
    4. No -- the diocese does not have a board of directors of
            Catholic Social Services (or of Catholic Charities)
    9. No response

FREQUENCIES:	General Population	1-10%	11-20%	21-30%	31-40%	41-50%
1.	62	13	14	12	11	6
2.	6	2	2	1	--	--
3.	1	--	1	--	--	--
4.	8	2	1	2	1	--
9.	2	2	--	--	--	--
MEAN:	1.416	1.471	1.389	1.467	1.250	1.000
MEDIAN:	1.121	1.154	1.143	1.125	1.136	1.000
MODE:	1.000	1.000	1.000	1.000	1.000	1.000
STD. DEV.:	.951	1.007	.850	1.060	.866	0

NOTE: The following question applied to #'s 95-100 below. "To what extent would the following qualities be important in a lay person serving on a board of directors of Catholic Social Services?"

95. Active in parish organizations

FREQUENCIES:	General Population	1-10%	11-20%	21-30%	31-40%	41-50%
1.	1	1	--	--	--	--
2.	15	2	5	2	4	--
3.	24	5	6	6	2	1
4.	23	4	4	4	5	5
5.	6	3	2	1	--	--
9.	10	4	1	2	1	--
MEAN:	3.261	3.400	3.176	3.308	3.091	3.833
MEDIAN:	3.271	3.400	3.083	3.250	3.250	3.900
MODE:	3.000	3.000	3.000	3.000	4.000	4.000
STD. DEV.:	.949	1.183	1.015	.855	.944	.408

96. Active in non-church community organizations

FREQUENCIES:	General Population	1-10%	11-20%	21-30%	31-40%	41-50%
1.	1	--	1	--	--	--
2.	13	2	6	2	1	1
3.	27	6	5	8	6	--
4.	24	6	4	3	2	5
5.	4	1	1	--	2	--
9.	10	4	1	2	1	--
MEAN:	3.246	3.400	2.882	3.077	3.455	3.667
MEDIAN:	3.259	3.417	2.800	3.063	3.250	3.800
MODE:	3.000	3.000	2.000	3.000	3.000	4.000
STD. DEV.:	.881	.828	1.054	.641	.934	.816

97. Have experience in other diocesan-wide committees and activities

FREQUENCIES:	General Population	1-10%	11-20%	21-30%	31-40%	41-50%
1.	2	--	2	--	--	--
2.	20	5	4	4	5	--
3.	29	7	8	7	1	1
4.	17	3	2	2	5	5
5.	1	--	1	--	--	--
9.	10	4	1	2	1	--
MEAN:	2.928	2.867	2.765	2.846	3.000	3.833
MEDIAN:	2.931	2.857	2.813	2.857	3.000	3.900
MODE:	3.000	3.000	3.000	3.000	2.000	4.000
STD. DEV.:	.846	.743	1.033	.689	1.000	.408

98. Are affiliated with other social service organizations

FREQUENCIES:	General Population	1-10%	11-20%	21-30%	31-40%	41-50%
1.	1	--	1	--	--	--
2.	15	2	6	2	4	--
3.	23	6	5	5	4	1
4.	25	6	5	5	1	4
5.	5	1	--	1	2	1
9.	10	4	1	2	1	--
MEAN:	3.261	3.400	2.824	3.385	3.091	4.000
MEDIAN:	3.304	3.417	2.800	3.400	2.875	4.000
MODE:	4.000	3.000	2.000	3.000	2.000	4.000
STD. DEV.:	.934	.828	.951	.870	1.136	.632

99. Are affiliated with important groups in the community

FREQUENCIES:	General Population	1-10%	11-20%	21-30%	31-40%	41-50%
1.	1	--	1	--	--	--
2.	11	2	4	1	2	--
3.	28	7	6	6	3	3
4.	19	4	2	6	3	3
5.	7	2	2	--	3	--
9.	13	4	3	2	1	--
MEAN:	3.303	3.400	3.000	3.385	3.636	3.500
MEDIAN:	3.250	3.286	2.917	3.417	3.667	5.000
MODE:	3.000	3.000	3.000	3.000	3.000	3.000
STD. DEV.:	.928	.910	1.134	.650	1.120	.548

100. Have knowledge and/or experience in the field of social work

FREQUENCIES:	General Population	1-10%	11-20%	21-30%	31-40%	41-50%
1.	1	--	--	--	1	--
2.	10	2	1	3	2	1
3.	20	3	4	5	5	2
4.	26	5	9	5	1	2
5.	11	5	2	--	2	1
9.	11	4	2	2	1	--
MEAN:	3.529	3.867	3.750	3.154	3.091	3.500
MEDIAN:	3.615	4.000	3.833	3.200	3.000	3.500
MODE:	4.000	4.000	4.000	3.000	3.000	3.000
STD. DEV.:	.985	1.060	.775	.801	1.221	1.049

101. To what extent are the expenses of Catholic Social Services covered by funds contributed directly by parishes?

1.	0-20%	4.	61-80%
2.	21-40%	5.	81-100%
3.	41-60%	9.	No response

FREQUENCIES:	General Population	1-10%	11-20%	21-30%	31-40%	41-50%
1.	49	10	15	9	8	5
2.	12	4	1	2	1	1
3.	2	--	--	1	--	--
4.	6	3	--	1	2	--
5.	4	1	1	--	--	--
9.	6	1	1	2	1	--
MEAN:	1.685	1.944	1.294	1.538	1.636	1.167
MEDIAN:	1.245	1.400	1.067	1.222	1.188	1.100
MODE:	1.000	1.000	1.000	1.000	1.000	1.000
STD. DEV.:	1.200	1.349	.985	.967	1.206	.408

102. To what extent are the   of Catholic Social Services covered by funds allocated by the diocese?

1.	0-20%	4.	61-80%
2.	21-40%	5.	81-100%
3.	41-60%	9.	No response

FREQUENCIES:	General Population	1-10%	11-20%	21-30%	31-40%	41-50%
1.	32	8	9	5	7	1
2.	14	2	4	1	3	2
3.	8	--	1	2	--	2
4.	10	6	--	2	1	1
5.	8	2	3	2	--	--
9.	7	1	1	3	1	--
MEAN:	2.278	2.556	2.059	2.583	1.545	2.500
MEDIAN:	1.786	2.000	1.444	2.500	1.286	2.500
MODE:	1.000	1.000	1.000	1.000	1.000	2.000
STD. DEV.:	1.436	1.617	1.519	1.621	.934	1.049

103. To what extent are the expenses of Catholic Social Services covered by funds from the United Way and similar agencies?

1.	0-20%	4.	61-80%
2.	21-40%	5.	81-100%
3.	41-60%	9.	No response

FREQUENCIES:	General Population	1-10%	11-20%	21-30%	31-40%	41-50%
1.	31	9	6	5	3	2
2.	20	4	3	5	4	2
3.	10	--	5	2	2	1
4.	12	4	3	1	2	1
5.	--	--	--	--	--	--
9.	6	1	1	2	1	--

MEAN:	2.041	2.056	2.294	1.923	2.273	2.167
MEDIAN:	1.775	1.500	2.333	1.800	2.125	2.000
MODE:	1.000	1.000	1.000	1.000	2.000	1.000
STD. DEV.:	1.111	1.305	1.160	.954	1.104	1.169

104. To what extent are the expenses of Catholic Social Services covered by fees charged for services?

1.	0-20%	4.	61-80%
2.	21-40%	5.	81-100%
3.	41-60%	9.	No response

FREQUENCIES:	General Population	1-10%	11-20%	21-30%	31-40%	41-50%
1.	55	15	10	9	9	6
2.	15	3	6	3	1	--
3.	3	--	1	1	1	--
4.	--	--	--	--	--	--
5.	--	--	--	--	--	--
9.	6	1	1	2	1	--

MEAN:	1.288	1.167	1.471	1.385	1.273	1.000
MEDIAN:	1.164	1.100	1.350	1.222	1.111	1.000
MODE:	1.000	1.000	1.000	1.000	1.000	1.000
STD. DEV.:	.540	.383	.624	.650	.647	0

105. To what extent are the expenses of Catholic Social Services covered by government support such as Federal Counseling Fees?

1.	0-20%	4.	61-80%
2.	21-40%	5.	81-100%
3.	41-60%	9.	No response

FREQUENCIES:	General Population	1-10%	11-20%	21-30%	31-40%	41-50%
1.	51	13	11	10	8	4
2.	15	5	4	2	1	2
3.	1	--	1	--	--	--
4.	2	--	--	1	--	--
5.	2	--	--	--	2	--
9.	8	1	2	2	1	--
MEAN:	1.437	1.278	1.375	1.385	1.818	1.333
MEDIAN:	1.196	1.192	1.227	1.150	1.188	1.250
MODE:	1.000	1.000	1.000	1.000	1.000	1.000
STD. DEV.:	.890	.461	.619	.870	1.601	.516

106. To what extent are the expenses of Catholic Social Services covered by direct contributions from business organizations in the community?

1.	0-20%	4.	61-80%
2.	21-40%	5.	81-100%
3.	41-60%	9.	No response

FREQUENCIES:	General Population	1-10%	11-20%	21-30%	31-40%	41-50%
1.	67	17	14	13	11	5
2.	4	--	3	--	--	1
3.	--	--	--	--	--	--
4.	--	--	--	--	--	--
5.	--	--	--	--	--	--
9.	8	2	1	2	1	--
MEAN:	1.056	1.000	1.176	1.000	1.000	1.167
MEDIAN:	1.030	1.000	1.107	1.000	1.000	1.100
MODE:	1.000	1.000	1.000	1.000	1.000	1.000
STD. DEV.:	.232	0	.393	0	0	.408

Notes

Chapter 1

1. Merle Severy, ed., *Great Religions of the World* (Washington, DC: National Geographic Society, 1978), 381.

2. Peter L. Berger and Richard John Neuhaus, *To Empower People: The Role of Mediating Structures in Public Policy* (Washington, DC: American Enterprise Institute for Public Policy Research, 1977), 28.

3. Max Weber, *The Protestant Ethic and the Spirit of Capitalism* (New York: Charles Scribner's Sons, 1958).

4. R.H. Tawney, *Religion and the Rise of Capitalism* (New York: Harcourt, Brace and Company, Inc., 1926).

5. Crane Brinton, John B. Christopher, and Robert Lee Wolff, *A History of Civilization* (Englewood Cliffs, NJ: Prentice-Hall, Inc., 1967), Vol. I., 120.

6. A.B.C. Whipple, *Fighting Sail* (Alexandrea, VA: Time-Life Books, 1978), 65.

7. Vern Terpstra, *The Cultural Environment of International Business* (Cincinnati, OH: South-Western Publishing Co., 1978), 28-59.

8. Janet P. Near, Robert W. Rice, and Raymond G. Hunt, "The Relationship Between Work and Nonwork Domains: A Review of Empirical Research," *The Academy of Management Review* 6(July 1980):415-29.

9. W.L. Thorkelson, "Judge Calls on Corporations to Repent," *Lutheran* 20(6 January 1982):21.

10. Peter L. Benson and Berton P. Strommen, "Religion on Capitol Hill: How Beliefs Affect Voting Behavior in the U.S. Congress," *Psychology Today* 15(December 1981):57.

11. Tai K. Oh and Moonsong David Oh, "The Influence of Confucianism on Japanese and Korean Management Practices: A Comparative Study" (Paper presented at the Annual Meeting of the Academy of International Business, Montreal, Quebec, Canada, 14-19 October 1981).

12. Kenneth E. Boulding, *Beyond Economics: Essays on Society, Religion, and Ethics* (Ann Arbor, MI: The University of Michigan Press, 1968), 198.

13. Berger and Neuhaus, *To Empower People*, 26-9.

14. Sol W. Sanders, "Iran's Victory Will Tip a Fragile Balance," *Business Week*, 22 March 1982, 54.

15. Asghar Fathi, "The Role of the Islamic Pupit," *Journal of Communications* 29(Summer 1979):102-3.

16. Frederick Kempe, "Polish Catholic Church Assumes Unifying Role with Warsaw's Assent," *Wall Street Journal*, 15 December 1982, 1,

17. Michael Dodson, "The Church in the Latin American Revolution: The Nicaraguan Case" (Paper presented at the conference on the Church and Society in Latin America, New Orleans, LA, 29-30 April 1982), 6,9.

18. Ernest McCrary, "A Political Time Bomb Imperils Brazil's New Stability," *Business Week*, 6 April 1982, 52.

19. Paul Blustein and Jane Mayer, "How the June Suicide of Ambrosiano's Chief Exposed a Murky Maze," *Wall Street Journal*, 30 August 1982, 1,6.

20. "LSTC Withdraws Account from Bank," *Lutheran* 20(6 January 1982):21.

21. Berger and Neuhaus, *To Empower People*, 26-29.

22. Jeffrey Pfeffer and Gerald R. Salancik, *The External Control of Organizations: A Resource Dependence Perspective* (New York: Harper & Row, 1978), 242-44.

23. Ibid., 144.

24. E. Yuchtman and S. Seashore, "A Systems Resource Approach to Organizational Effect," *American Sociological Review* 32(December 1967):891-903.

Chapter 2

1. Msgr. John P. Kleinz, *The Development of Catholic Social Doctrine from Pope Leo XIII to Pope John Paul II* (Columbus, OH: Pontifical College Josephinum, 1979), 10.

2. Pope John Paul II, "Laborem Exercens," *National Catholic Reporter*, 25 September 1981, 23.

3. "John Paul Quoted on Various Topics," *Indianapolis Star*, 14 May 1981, 15.

4. John Paul II, "Laborem Exercens," 14.

5. Adam Smith, *The Wealth of Nations*, books I-III, Andrew Skinner, ed. (New York: Penguin Books, 1978), 139-40.

6. George W. Wilson, ed., *Classics of Economic Theory* (Bloomington, IN.: Indiana University Press, 1964), 604-8.

7. Karl Marx, *Capital: A Critique of Political Economy*, vol. I (New York: Vintage Books, 1977), 38-46.

8. Karl Marx and Friedrich Engels, *The Communist Manifesto* (New York: Penguin Books, 1979), 87.

9. Marx, *Capital*, 1083-84.

10. Ibid., 885.

11. Ibid., 171.

12. Kleinz, *The Development of Catholic Social Doctrine*, 15.

13. *Pope John Paul II at the United Nations* (New York: United Nations Publication, 1980), 43-44.

14. Eric Roll, *A History of Economic Thought* (Boston: Faber & Faber, Ltd., 1978), 20-21.

15. Ibid., 20.

16. Ibid., 22-23.

17. Ibid.

18. Ibid.

19. Ibid., 24.

20. Ibid., 27-31.

21. Ibid., 27.

22. Ibid., 31.

23. Ibid., 32.

24. Ibid., 31-32.

25. An interesting illustration of how pervasive Aristotle's ideas were and of the impact they had on scholars in the Middle Ages may be seen in the importance this theory of natural slavery was given later in a debate over treatment of the American Indians which took place in Spain in 1550 and 1551. Almost 1,900 years after his death, Aristotle's doctrine of natural slavery was central to the arguments in a debate between Bartolomé de las Casas, a Spanish Dominican, and John Gines de Sepúlveda, a Renaissance scholar. See: Lewis Hanke, *Aristotle and the American Indians: A Study in Race Prejudice in the Modern World* (Bloomington, IN: Indiana University Press, 1975), 1, 16-18.

26. Roll, *A History of Economic Thought*, 31.

27. Wilson, *Classics of Economic Theory*, 13.

28. Ibid., 14.

29. Roll, *A History of Economic Thought*, 38.

30. Wilson, *Classic of Economic Theory*, 13.

31. Crane Brinton, John B. Christopher, and Robert Lee Wolff, *A History of Civilization*, vol. I (Englewood Cliffs, NJ: Prentice-Hall, Inc., 1967), 53.

32. Wilson, *Classics of Economic Theory*, 13-15.

33. Ibid., 15.

34. Roll, *A History of Economic Thought*, 35.

35. Ibid., 36-37.

36. Ibid., 38.

37. Ibid., 38-40.

38. Ibid., 40.

39. Alfred Weber, *History of Philosophy* (New York: Charles Scribner's Sons, 1925), 154-56.

40. Wilson, *Classics of Economic Theory*, 14-15.

41. Ibid., 15.

42. Jeffrey Rose and Michael Ignatieff, eds., *Religion and International Affairs* (Toronto: House of Auansi Press, 1968), 23-33.

43. Pierre Bigo, *The Church and Third World Revolution* (Maryknoll, NY: Orbis Books, 1977), 120-21.

44. John W. Clark, S.J., *Religion and the Moral Standards of American Businessmen* (Cincinnati, OH: South-Western Publishing Co., 1966), 62.

45. Barbara W. Tuchman, *A Distant Mirror: The Calamitous 14th Century* (New York: Ballantine Books, 1978), 6.

46. Ibid.

47. Ibid., 173.

48. Jack Melitz and Donald Winch, eds., *Religious Thought and Economic Society: Four Chapters of an Unfinished Work by Jacob Viner* (Durham, NC: Duke University Press, 1978), 17.

49. Brinton, et al., *A History of Civilization*, 314.

50. Melitz and Winch, *Religious Thought and Economic Society*, 18-20.

51. Ibid., 21,25.

52. Ibid., 20-21.

53. Ibid., 26-27.

54. Ibid., 31-32.

55. Ibid., 23.

56. Ibid., 34-38.

57. Roll, *A History of Economic Thought*, 43.

58. Melitz and Winch, *Religious Thought and Economic Society*, 38-39.

59. Ibid., 42.

60. Ibid., 49-51.

61. Ibid., 24.

62. Ibid., 43.

63. Ibid.

64. Ibid., 44.

65. Ibid., 48.

66. Herbert J. Muller, *The Uses of the Past* (New York: Oxford University Press, 1957), 254.

67. George W. Wilson, "The Economics of Just Price," *History of Political Economy* (Spring 1975): 56.

68. Alfred Weber, *History of Philosophy*, 185-86.

69. Wilson, *Classics of Economic Theory*, 16-17.

70. Wilson, "The Economics of Just Price," 61.

71. Ibid., 58.

72. Pope John Paul II, "Laborem Exercens," 13.

73. Wilson, "The Economics of Just Price," 65.

74. Wilson, *Classics of Economic Theory*, 17.

75. Ibid.

76. Ibid.

77. Ibid., 14-15.

78. Roll, *A History of Economic Thought*, 48.

79. Muller, *The Uses of the Past*, 251.

80. David Hollenbach, S.J., "Both Bread and Freedom: The Interconnection of Economic and Political Rights in Recent Catholic Thought" (Paper presented at the American Enterprise Institute's Summer Insititute, Washington, DC, 7-9 July 1981), 9.

81. Melitz and Winch, *Religious Thought and Economic Society*, 63.

82. Ibid., 50-51.

83. Ibid., 67-73.

84. Roll, *A History of Economic Thought*, 53.

85. Alfred Weber, *History of Philosophy*, 194-95.

86. Melitz and Winch, *Religious Thought and Economic Society*, 106.

87. Roll, *A History of Economic Thought*, 54.

88. Melitz and Winch, *Religious Thought and Economic Society*, 111-13.

89. Alfred Weber, *History of Philosophy*, 157.

90. Roll, *A History of Economic Thought*, 53.

91. Ibid.

92. Clark, *Religion and the Moral Standards of American Businessmen*, 68.

93. Ibid., 69.

94. Wilson, *Classics of Economic Theory*, 19.

95. Roll, *A History of Economic Thought*, 62-63.

96. Ibid., 57-58.

97. Ibid., 56-57.

98. Wilson, *Classics of Economic Theory*, 19.

99. Roll, *A History of Economic Thought*, 74.

100. Ibid., 79.

101. Ibid., 85.

102. Ibid., 91.

103. Ibid., 90-91.

104. Ibid., 91.

105. Ibid.

106. Ibid., 130.

107. Ibid., 114.

108. Wilson, *Classics of Economic Theory*, 20-22.

109. Ibid., 22.

110. Roll, *A History of Economic Thought*, 23.

111. Wilson, *Classics of Economic Theory*, 23.

112. Roll, *A History of Economic Thought*, 150.

113. Ibid., 151.

114. Adam Smith, *The Wealth of Nations*, 150.

115. Ibid., 151.

116. Ibid., 157-58.

117. Ibid., 160.

118. Ibid., 165-66.

119. Wilson, *Classics of Economic Theory*, 244-45.

120. Ibid., 249-53.

121. Ibid., 253-58.

122. Ibid., 27.

123. Ibid.

124. Ibid., 301-5.

125. Ibid., 232-37.

126. Ibid., 28.

127. Ibid., 328-29.

128. Ibid., 363-73.

129. Ibid., 28.

130. Roll, *A History of Economic Thought*, 287.

131. Marx, *Capital*, 725-34.

132. Ibid., 873-76.

133. Joseph A. Schumpeter, *Capitalism, Socialism, and Democracy* (New York: Harper and Brothers Publishers, 1947), 197.

134. Wilson, *Classics of Economic Theory*, 350-52.

135. Ibid., 352.

136. Ibid., 357-58.

137. Some have argued that Marxian value was a matter of definition rather than theory, that he never claimed to have a labor theory of value and to some extent, tried to separate his work from close links with Ricardo's. See: Thomas Sowell, "Marx's *Capital* After One Hundred Years," *Canadian Journal of Economics and Political Science* (February 1967):67-68. Nevertheless, most writers take the position that Marx's theory of value was basically Ricardo's labor jelly theory and that is the position accepted for purposes of this research.

138. Wilson, *Classics of Economic Theory*, 29.

139. Ibid., 30.

140. Ibid., 31.

141. Ibid., 32.

142. Ibid., 545-49.

143. Ibid., 549.

144. Ibid., 555-56.

145. Ibid., 589.

146. Ibid., 612-13.

147. Ibid., 636.

148. Breit and Ransom, *The Academic Scribblers: American Economists in Collision* (New York: Holt, Rinehard and Winston, Inc., 1971), 73-76.

149. Kleinz, *The Development of Catholic Social Doctrine*.

150. Rev. Gerald C. Treacy, ed., *Five Great Encyclicals* (New York: The Paulist Press, 1953), 11.

151. Hollenbach, "Both Bread and Freedom," 7-9.

152. Reverend John D. Callahan, *The Catholic Attitude Toward a Familial Minimum Wage* (Washington, DC: Murry and Heister, 1936), 24-25.

153. Ibid., 25.

154. Ibid., 128.

155. R.R. Palmer and Joel Colton, *A History of the Modern World* (New York: Alfred A. Knopf, 1969), 38.

156. Treacy, *Five Great Encyclicals*, 2.

157. Ibid., 3-7.

158. Ibid., 18,20.

159. Stephen J. Tonsor, "The Medieval Model of Social Reconstruction and the 19th and 20th Century Reality" (Paper presented at the American Enterprise Institute's Summer Institute, Washington, DC, 7-9 July 1981), 5.

160. Ibid.

161. Ibid., 7.

162. Ibid., 4.

163. Peter Nichols, *The Pope's Divisions: The Roman Catholic Church Today* (New York: Holt, Rinehart and Winston, 1981), 284.

164. Ibid., 282.

165. Treacy, *Five Great Encyclicals*, 137.

166. Ibid., 139.

167. Ibid., 141.

168. Ibid., 145-46.

169. Kleinz, *The Development of Catholic Social Doctrine*, 15.

170. William J. Givvons, S.J. (Translator), *Mater et Magistra: Encyclical Letter of His Holiness Pope John XXIII* (Glen Rock, NJ: Paulist Press, 1962), 29.

171. Ibid., 30-32.

172. Ibid., 40-41.

173. Kleinz, *The Development of Catholic Social Doctrine*, 19.

174. Ibid., 21.

175. John Paul II, "Laborem Exercens," 13.

176. Ibid., 12.

177. Ibid.

178. "John Paul Quoted on Various Topics," 15.

179. John Paul II, "Laborem Exercens," 14.

180. Kleinz, *The Development of Catholic Social Doctrine*, 22.

181. Arthur F. McGovern, *Marxism: An American Christian Perspective* (Maryknoll, NY: Orbis Books, 1980), 93.

182. Ibid., 103-5.

183. Ibid., 105.

184. Ibid., 106.

185. Ibid., 110.

186. Nichols, *The Pope's Divisions*, 286.

187. John Paul II, "Laborem Exercens," 13.

188. McGovern, *Marxism*, 115.

189. Nichols, *The Pope's Divisions*, 286.

190. McGovern, *Marxism*, 110.

191. Nichols, *The Pope's Divisions*, 174-85.

192. Ibid., 18,23.

193. Ibid., 43.

194. Ibid., 48.

195. Ibid.

196. Ibid., 43.

197. Walter M. Abbot, S.J., ed., *The Documents of Vatican II* (New York: Herder and Herder, 1966), 408.

198. Ibid., 412-14.

199. Ibid., 416-17.

200. Nichols, *The Pope's Divisions*, 44.

201. Ibid., 161, 164, 167.

202. Ibid., 44.

203. Wilson, *Classics of Economic Theory*, 29.

204. John Paul II, "Laborem Exercens," 13.

205. Barry Keating and Maryann Keating, "The Treatment of Labor in Economic Theory and Practice" (Paper presented at the conference, Co-Creation: A Religious Vision of Corporate Power, South Bend, IN, 3-5 May 1982), 2-3.

206. Wilson, *Classics of Economic Theory*, 17.

207. McGovern, *Marxism*, 113-17, 136, 172.

208. Jeffrey Pfeffer and Gerald R. Salancik, *The External Control of Organizations: A Resource Dependence Perspective* (New York: Harper & Row, 1978), 192.

209. Nichols, *The Pope's Divisions*, 333.

210. Ibid., 337.

211. Ibid.

212. Ibid., 339-40.

213. Ibid., 337.

214. Ibid., 339.

215. "Nestlé to Tighten Formula Rules," *Saint Louis Post-Dispatch*, 1 October 1982, 16A.

216. Charles G. Robertson, Jr., "The Special Relationship of the Church in Poland to the Dissident Movement" (unpublished manuscript), 7.

217. Neil Ulman, "Church and Labor Seek 'Just Society' in Brazil as Key Elections Near," *Wall Street Journal*, 21 September 1982, 1,22.

218. Rose and Ignatieff, *Religion and International Affairs*, 36-37.

219. "John Paul Quoted on Various Topics," 15.

220. William Buckley, "Meanwhile in the Seminaries," *Herald-Telephone* (Bloomington, IN), 17 July 1982, 5.

221. Nichols, *The Pope's Divisions*, 358-70.

222. Ibid., 286.

Chapter 3

1. This chart is a combination of information from: 1) Peter Nichols, *The Pope's Divisions: The Roman Catholic Church Today* (New York: Holt, Rinehart and Winston, 1981); 2) *The Official Catholic Directory* (New York: P.J. Kenedy & Sons, 1982); and 3) interview of church officials by the author.

2. Nichols, *The Pope's Divisions*, 166-70.

3. Ibid., 154.

4. Ibid., 160.

5. Ibid., 164-65.

6. Ibid., 166-70.

7. Ibid., 154.

8. Ibid., 162.

9. Ibid., 120-21.

10. Ibid., 123.

11. This chart is based primarily on interviews with officials of the Archdiocese of Indianapolis and the Diocese of Lafayette, Indiana; on literature put out by these two dioceses; on questionnaire data; and, to a limited extent, on other published data.

Chapter 4

1. Gregory Baum and Andrew Greeley, ed., *The Church as Institution* (New York: Herder and Herder, 1974), 140-41.

2. Ibid., 109-18.

3. Ibid., 125-26.

4. Johannes B. Metz, *Faith in the World of Politics* (New York: Paulist Press, 1968), 95.

5. Peter Nichols, *The Pope's Divisions: The Roman Catholic Church Today* (New York: Holt, Rinehart and Winston), 21-39.

6. Baum and Greeley, *The Church as Institution*, 143.

7. Jeffrey Pfeffer and Gerald R. Salancik, *The External Control of Organizations: A Resource Dependence Perspective* (New York: Harper & Row, 1978).

8. Ibid., 242-44.

9. Ibid., 168.

10. Albert J. Reiss, Jr. et al., *Occupations and Social Status* (New York: The Free Press of Glencoe, Inc., 1961), 122-23.

Chapter 5

1. Albert J. Reiss, Jr., et. al., *Occupations and Social Status* (New York: The Free Press of Glencoe, Inc., 1961), 122-23.

2. Jeffrey Pfeffer, "Size, Composition and Function of Hospital Boards of Directors: A Study of Organization-Environment Linkage." *Administrative Science Quarterly* 18 (September 1973):349-64.

Chapter 6

1. Barry M. Staw and Eugene Szwajkowski, "The Scarcity-Munificence Component of Organizational Environments and the Commission of Illegal Acts," *Administrative Science Quarterly* 20(September 1975):345-54.

2. John B. Miner, *Theories of Organizational Structure and Process* (Chicago: The Dryden Press, 1982), 179.

Chapter 7

1. James Thompson, ed., *Approaches to Organizational Design* (Pittsburgh, PA: University of Pittsburgh Press, 1966):70.

2. Delbert C. Miller, Eva Chamorro, and Juan Carlos Agulla, "Community Power Perspectives and Role Definitions of North American Executives in an Argentine Community," *Administrative Science Quarterly* 10(December, 1965):364-80.

Glossary

Abbot: A man who is head of an abbey of monks.

Apostolic Delegate: The representative of the Vatican sent to a country which has not established diplomatic relations with the papacy.

Archbishop: A bishop of the highest rank who presides over an archbishopric or metropolitan see. An archbishop has no formal authority over other bishops in matters pertaining to their individual dioceses.

Area Vicar: In some dioceses, a term used to refer to priests serving in the capacity of deans.

Aston Studies: Important studies of organization structure carried out by Derek Pugh and his associates at the University of Aston in Birmingham, England.

Auxiliary Bishop: In a very large diocese, a prelate who assists the bishop. An auxiliary bishop does not have the right to succeed the bishop and does not enjoy ordinary authority.

Bishop: A prelate who usually oversees a number of parishes. A member of the highest order in the priesthood.

Boundary Spanning: A term used in management and organization theory to designate activities which link an organization to its environment (e.g., public relations, purchasing, marketing, legal department). Persons acting in such a capacity are referred to as boundary spanners.

Canon Law: The law of the Roman Catholic church.

Cardinal: The title given to one who may participate in the election of the pope. In the past this was not necessarily limited to members of the priesthood but today it is essentially an office conferred only on selected bishops. About half of all cardinals serve in Rome in the administration of the church while somewhat more than half are ordinaries in dioceses. Cardinals are often referred to as "princes of the church."

Chancellor: After the bishop, the chief administrative officer for religious matters in a diocese.

Chancery: The primary office in a diocese with responsibility for overseeing administration in religious matters.

Coadjutor Bishop: In a very large diocese, a prelate who assists the bishop and has the right to succeed the bishop as ordinary. A coadjutor bishop does not enjoy ordinary authority.

Curia: The nine sacred congregations made up primarily of cardinals in Rome which assist the pope to administer the church.

Dean: A senior priest appointed by the bishop to act as the bishop's representative to several parishes within the diocese. In the bishop's absence a dean may perform some of the episcopal functions.

Diocese: A geographic division of the church composed of several parishes. The seat of a bishop (the Archdiocese of Indianapolis includes more than 160 parishes).

Diocesan Consultors: A group of priests who serve as advisors to the ordinary of a diocese. With the advent of priests' senates in the United States the function of consultors has become much less important, although they often serve to coordinate the process of seeking a new bishop when necessary.

Diocesan Priest: A priest who holds his appointment within a specific diocese (as opposed to a priest whose affiliation is with a religious order).

Diocesan Tribunal: An office which adjudicates cases within a diocese which involve questions of religious justice. Currently, this office is frequently referred to as the "marriage tribunal," as the vast majority of cases brought to it are concerned with the annulment of marriages.

Episcopal: Having to do with or at the level of bishops.

International Synod of Bishops: Established in 1965 by Pope Paul VI, a body of bishops, chosen by the national episcopal conferences, which meets in Rome once every three years for the purpose of consulting with the pope.

Juridical: As used in this book, recognized in canon law.

Men Religious: A general term used to refer to men who are members of religious orders.

Metropolitan: Another term used to refer to an archbishop.

Metropolitan See: The seat of an archbishop. A term used synonymously with archbishopric.

Monsignor: An honor conferred by Rome on priests for long and/or distinguished service to the church. A monsignor has no additional authority as a result of this appointment but often, as a result of long service, will hold a post of authority, such as dean, as well.

National Episcopal Conferences: Bodies of bishops within individual countries or regions which meet to consider theological concerns. In the United States this is the National Conference of Catholic Bishops.

New Curia: The secretariats (including the secretariat of state) which have been set up in recent times and which, in addition to the nine sacred congregations of the curia, assist the pope to administer the church.

Ordinary: A title frequently used to refer to the bishop who holds final authority in a diocese.

Ordinary Authority: The formal authority which is possessed by an individual who has final or absolute authority within a given unit of the church. The bishop in a diocese or the senior priest in a parish have ordinary authority within those units.

Papal Nuncio: The representative of the Vatican sent to a country which has established official diplomatic ties with the papacy.

Parish: The geographic area served by a specific church.

Parish Council: A body composed of representatives of parishioners who advise and consult with the parish priest (similar to the role of the pastoral council at a diocesan level).

Pastoral Council: A body composed of priests, lay people, and representatives of religious orders which advises and consults with the bishop of a diocese. At the present time pastoral councils exist in about half of all U.S. dioceses.

Peter's Pence: An offering given by the people of the entire Catholic church, through the dioceses, every 29 July (the feast of St. Peter and St. Paul) which is a major source of Vatican funds.

Pope: Title of the head of the church who is the bishop of Rome.

Prefect: As used in this book, the title given to a cardinal who leads one of the sacred congregations.

Priests' Senate: A body made up entirely of priests from a diocese which advises and consults with the bishop.

Primacial See: Dioceses, such as Baltimore, which were established early in U.S. history and are frequently the seat of a cardinal (very large dioceses, such as Chicago, may not be primacial sees but, due to their size, are often also seats of cardinals).

Province: A group of adjacent dioceses which may coordinate efforts on some issues. In the United States these frequently follow state borders, such as the Province of Indiana, which is composed of the Archdiocese of Indianapolis and the Dioceses of Lafayette, Gary, Evansville, and Fort Wayne-South Bend. Meetings of the bishops of the province will normally be called by the archbishop.

Roman Tribunal: The "Supreme Court" of the church. Acts as a court for the interpretation of canon law and provides for the establishment of regional tribunals.

Secretariat of State: The central administrative office of the Vatican and a critical link between the Pope and the national churches through its appointment and contact with Papal Nuncios and Apostolic Delegates. Part of the "New Curia," it coordinates most of the activities of the other offices and congregations.

Substitute and Secretary of the Cypher: The title given to the assistant to the cardinal-secretary of state of the Roman Catholic church.

Superior: The head of a religious community.

Vatican: As used in this book, the authority and government of the pope.

Vatican II: The name of the twenty-first ecumenical council of bishops held from 1962 to 1965 at the Vatican. It is credited with significant reforms in the church and, in particular, with opening the church to more of its own members, to other Christians, and to the world at large.

Vicar: A title given to priests who assist the bishop in administering a diocese. In some dioceses the title of dean is given to these individuals.

Vicar General: A priest who acts in the capacity of "assistant bishop." In dioceses which have a coadjutor or an auxiliary bishop this individual is automatically designated vicar general.

Women Religious: A general term used to refer to women who are members of religious orders.

Bibliography

Abbott, Walter M., ed. *The Documents of Vatican II.* New York: Herder and Herder Association Press, 1966.

Akey, Denise S. *Encyclopedia of Associations.* Vol. 1. Detroit, MI: Gale Research Co., 1981.

Aldrich, Howard E. *Organizations and Environments.* Englewood Cliffs, NJ: Prentice-Hall, Inc., 1979.

Allen, Michael Patrick. "The Structure of Interorganizational Elite Cooptation: Interlocking Corporate Directorates." *American Sociological Review* 39(June 1974):393-406.

Aplin, John C. and Hegarty, W. Harvey. "Political Influence: Strategies Employed by Organizations to Impact Legislation in Business and Economic Matters." *Academy of Management Journal* 23(September 1980):438-50.

Bauer, P.T. "Ecclesiastical Economics: Envy Enthroned." Paper presented at the Summer 1981 American Enterprise Institute Workshop, Washington, 7-9 July 1981.

Baum, Gregory and Greely, Andrew. *The Church as Institution.* New York: Herder and Herder, 1974.

_____. *Communication in the Church.* New York: The Seabury Press, 1978.

Benson, Peter L., and Strommen, Merton P. "Religion on Capitol Hill." *Psychology Today* 15(December 1981):46-57.

Berger, Peter L. and Neuhaus, Richard John. *To Empower People: The Role of Mediating Structures in Public Policy.* Washington, DC: American Enterprise Institute for Public Policy Research, 1977.

Bergstein, C. Fred; Horst, Thomas; and Moran, Theodore H. *American Multinationals and American Interests.* Washington, DC: The Brookings Institute, 1978.

Bigo, Pierre. *The Church and Third World Revolution.* Maryknoll, NY: Orbis Books, 1977.

Blustein, Paul. "Maryknoll Missionaries Draw Praise, Criticism for Social Involvement." *Wall Street Journal* (14 August 1981):1, 13.

_____, and Mayer, Jane. "How the June Suicide of Ambrosiano's Chief Exposed a Murky Maze." *Wall Street Journal* (30 August 1982):1, 6.

Boulding, Kenneth E. *Beyond Economics.* Ann Arbor, MI: The University of Michigan Press, 1968.

Breit, William and Ransom, Roger L. *The Academic Scribblers: American Economists in Collision.* New York: Holt, Rinehart and Winston, Inc., 1971.

Brinton, Crane, Christopher, John B., and Wolff, Robert Lee. *A History of Civilization.* Vol. 1. Englewood Cliffs, NJ: Prentice-Hall, Inc., 1967.

Buckley, William. "Meanwhile, in the Seminaries." *Herald-Telephone,* Bloomington, Indiana (17 July 1982):5.

Callahan, Reverend John D. *The Catholic Attitude Toward a Familial Minimum Wage.* Washington, DC: Murray & Heister, 1936.

Child, John. "Organization Structure, Environment, and Performance—The Role of Strategic Choice." *Sociology* 11 (January 1972):1-22.

Childs, Marquis W., and Cater, Douglass. *Ethics in a Business Society.* New York: Harper and Brothers, 1954.

"The Church's Unholy Alliance in Latin America." *Business Week* (9 March 1981):44-46.

Clark, John W. *Religion and the Moral Standards of American Businessmen.* Cincinnati, OH: South-Western Publishing Co., 1966.

Cohn, Norman. *The Pursuit of the Millennium.* New York: Oxford University Press, 1970.

Cyert, Richard M., and March, James G. *A Behavioral Theory of the Firm.* Englewood Cliffs, NJ: Prentice-Hall, Inc., 1963.

Dahl, Gordon J. "Work, Play and Worship—Toward a New Moral Economy." *Journal of Health, Physical Education, Recreation* (November-December 1974): 38-40.

Davis, Charles. *Theology and Political Society.* New York: Cambridge University Press, 1978.

Derr, Thomas Sieger. "The Economic Thought of the World Council of Churches." Paper presented at the Summer 1981 American Enterprise Institute Workshop, Washington, DC, 7-9 July 1981.

Dodson, Michael. "The Church in the Latin American Revolution: The Nicaraguan Case." Paper presented at the Conference on the Church and Society in Latin America, New Orleans, LA, 29-30 April 1982.

————. "Religious Innovation and the Politics of Argentina: A Study of the Movement of Priests for the Third World." Ph.D. Dissertation, Indiana University, 1973.

Dominguez, Jorge I., Rodley, Nigel S., Wood, Bryce, and Falk, Richard. *Enhancing Global Human Rights.* New York: McGraw-Hill Book Company, 1979.

Dooley, Peter. "The Interlocking Directorate." *American Economic Review* 59(June 1969):314-23.

Emery, F.E., and Trist, E.L. "The Causal Texture of Organizational Environments." In *Readings in Organization Theory: Open Systems Approaches,* edited by John G. Maurer. New York: Random House, 1971.

Evan, William M. "The Organization-Set: Toward a Theory of Interorganizational Relations." In *Complex Organizations and Their Environments,* edited by Merlin B. Brinkerhoff and Philip R. Kunz. Dubuque, IA: W.C. Brown Company, 1972.

Fathi, Asghar. "The Role of the Islamic Pulpit." *Journal of Communications* 29(Summer 1979):102-6.

Fichter, Joseph H. *Organization Man in the Church.* Cambridge, MA: Schenkman Publishing Co., 1974.

Finn, James. "Religion and Economics." *Worldview* (August 1981):4-6.

Flynn, E. James. "The Resource Dependence and Population Ecology Model: A Literature Review." Unpublished paper, Indiana University, 1982.

Ford, Jeffrey D. "The Administrative Component in Growing and Declining Organizations: A Longitudinal Analysis." *Academy of Management Journal* 23(December 1980):615-30.

Gable, R.W. "NAM: Influential Lobby or Kiss of Death?" *Journal of Politics* 15(May 1953):254-73.

Getschow, George. "Mexico's Old Rivalry of Church and State Lingers Despite Truce." *Wall Street Journal* (21 July 1981):1, 16.

Givvons, William J., trans. *Mater et Magistra: Encyclical Letter of His Holiness Pope John XXIII.* Glen Rock, NJ: Paulist Press, 1962.

Gongora, Mario. *Studies in the Colonial History of Spanish America.* London: Cambridge University Press, 1975.

Greeley, Andrew M. *Uncertain Trumpet: The Priest in Modern America.* New York: Sheed and Ward, 1968.

Hall, Douglas T. and Schneider, Benjamin. *Organizational Climates and Careers: The Work Lives of Priests.* New York: Seminar Press, 1973.

Handelman, Howard. *Ecuadorian Agrarian Reform: The Politics of Limited Change.* Hanover, New Hampshire: American Universities Field Staff, 1980 (No. 49, H-2-'80).

_____. *Peasants, Landlords, and Bureaucrats: The Politics of Agrarian Reform in Peru.* Hanover, New Hampshire: American Universities Field Staff, 1981 (No. 1, HH-1-'81).

Handy, Robert T. *A History of the Churches in the United States and Canada.* New York: Oxford University Press, 1979.

Hanke, Lewis. *Aristotle and the American Indians: A Study in Race Prejudice in the Modern World.* Bloomington, IN: Indiana University Press, 1975.

Haring, Clarence Henry. *The Spanish Empire in America.* New York: Oxford University Press, 1947.

Hinings, C.R., Ranson, S., and Bryman, A. "Churches as Organizations: Structure and Context." In *Organizational Structure, Extensions and Replications: The Aston Programme II,* edited by D.S. Pugh and C.R. Hinings. Westmead, England: Saxon House, Teakfield, Limited, 1976.

Hirsch, P.M. "Organizational Effectiveness and the Institutional Environment." *Administrative Science Quarterly* 20(September 1975):327-44.

Hollenbach, David. "Both Bread and Freedom: The Interconnection of Economic and Political Rights in Recent Catholic Thought." Paper presented at the Summer 1981 American Enterprise Institute, Washington, DC, 7-9 July 1981.

Ignatius, David. "Egypt's Religious Strife Raises Prospect of Yet Another Trouble Spot in Mideast." *Wall Street Journal* (7 August 1981):18.

_____. "Struggle in Islam: Egypt's Path Depends in Part on Bid to Curb its Moslem Extremists." *Wall Street Journal* (9 October 1981):1, 18.

"John Paul Quoted on Various Topics." *Indianapolis Star* (14 May 1981):15.

Keating, Barry, and Keating, Maryann. "The Treatment of Labor in Economic Theory and Practice." Paper presented at the conference: Co-Creation—A Religious Vision of Corporate Power, 3-5 May 1982, South Bend, IN.

Kelley, Lane, and Worthley, Reginald. "The Role of Culture in Comparative Management: A Cross Cultural Perspective." *Academy of Management Journal* 24(March 1981):164-73.

Kempe, Frederick. "Polish Catholic Church Assumes Unifying Role With Warsaw's Assent." *Wall Street Journal* (15 December 1981):1, 19.

Kleinz, John P. *The Development of Catholic Social Doctrine from Pope Leo XIII to Pope John Paul II.* Columbus, OH: Office of Continuing Education for Priests, Diocese of Columbus, 1979.

Lernoux, Penny. "Latin American Catholics: A Force for Change." *Louisville Courier-Journal* (21 June 1981): 1, 4D.

Levine, Daniel H. *Conflict and Political Change in Venezuela.* Princeton, NJ: Princeton University Press, 1973.

Littlejohn, Edward. "Papal Teachings on the Economy." Paper presented at the Summer 1981 American Enterprise Institute Workshop, Washington, DC, 7-9 July 1981.

Litwak, E., and Hylton, L.F. "Interorganizational Analysis: A Hypothesis on Coordinating Agencies." *Administrative Science Quarterly* 6(March 1962):395-420.

Lombardi, John V. "Latin America and Eastern Europe: The Response to the Multinational." Unpublished draft, Indiana University, March 1981.

Long, John D. "The Protestant Ethic Reexamined." *Business Horizons* (February 1972).

"LSTC Withdraws Account from Bank." *Lutheran* (6 January 1982):21.

McBrien, Richard P. *Catholicism—Study Edition.* Minneapolis, MN: Winston Press, 1981.

McCrary, Ernest. "A Political Time Bomb Imperils Brazil's New Stability." *Business Week* (6 April 1982):52.

McGovern, Arthur F. *Marxism: An American Christian Perspective.* Maryknoll, NY: Orbis Books, 1980.

Malloy, James M., ed. *Authoritarianism and Corporatism in Latin America.* Pittsburgh, PA: University of Pittsburgh Press, 1977.

Martz, John D., and Myers, David J., eds. *Venezuela: The Democratic Experience.* New York: Praeger Publishers, 1977.

Marx, Karl. *Capital.* New York: Vintage Books, 1977.

_____, and Engels, Friedrich. *The Communist Manifesto.* New York: Penguin Books, 1979.

Mazrui, Ali A. "The Barrel of the Gun and the Barrel of Oil in North-South Equation." Working Paper Number Five, World Order Models Project. NY: Institute for World Order, 1978.

Metz, Johannes B. *Faith and the World of Politics.* New York: Paulist Press, 1968.

Meyer, Roger A. "Multivariate Analysis of Social and Religious Attitudes." Paper presented at the 84th Annual Meeting of the American Psychological Association, Washington, DC, 4 September 1976.

Miller, Delbert C., Chamorro, Eva, and Agulla, Juan Carlos. "Community Power Perspectives and Role Definitions of North American Executives in an Argentine Community." *Administrative Science Quarterly* 10(December 1964):364-80.

Miner, John B. *Theories of Organizational Structure and Process.* Chicago: The Dryden Press, 1982.

Moorman, Paul. "The Golden Age of Islamic Education." *Change* 10(March 1978):13-17.

Muller, Herbert J. *The Uses of the Past.* New York: Oxford University Press, 1957.

Near, Janet P., Rice, Robert W., and Hunt, Raymond G. "The Relationship Between Work and Nonwork Domains: A Review of Empirical Research." *Academy of Management Review* 5(July 1980):415-29.

"Nestle to Tighten Formula Rules." *Saint Louis Post-Dispatch* (1 October 1982):16A.

Nichols, Peter. *The Pope's Divisions: The Roman Catholic Church Today.* New York: Holt, Rinehart and Winston, 1981.

The Official Catholic Directory. New York: P.J. Kenedy & Sons, 1982.

Oh, Tai K., and Oh, Moonsong David. "The Influence of Confucianism on Japanese and Korean Management Practices: A Comparative Study." Paper presented at the Academy of International Business Annual Conference, Montreal, Quebec, Canada, 14-19 October 1981.

Ornstein, Michael. "The Boards and Executives of the Largest Canadian Corporations: Size, Composition, and Interlocks." *Canadian Journal of Sociology* 1(Winter 1976):411-37.

Ostling, Richard. "Those Beleaguered Maryknollers." *Time* (6 July 1981):36-37.

Palmer, R.R., and Colton, Joel. *A History of the Modern World.* New York: Alfred A. Knopf, 1969.

Pennings, Johannes M. "Strategically Interdependent Organizations." In *Handbook of Organizational Design,* edited by Paul G. Nystrom and William H. Starbuck. Amsterdam, The Netherlands: Elsevier Scientific, Forthcoming.

Perrow, Charles. *Organizational Analysis: A Sociological View.* Monterey, CA: Brooks/Cole Publishing Company, 1970.

Pfeffer, Jeffrey. "Size and Composition of Corporate Boards of Directors." *Administrative Science Quarterly* 17(June 1972):218-28.

_____. "Size, Composition, and Function of Hospital Boards of Directors: A Study of Organization-Environment Linkage." *Administrative Science Quarterly* 18(September 1973):349-64.

_____, and Salancik, Gerald R. *The External Control of Organizations: A Resource Dependence Perspective.* New York: Harper & Row, Publishers, 1978.

Pope John Paul II. "Laborem Exercens." *National Catholic Reporter* (25 September 1981):11-26.

"Pope Stresses Dignity of Workers in Speech at Italian Steel Plant." *Indianapolis Star* (20 March 1981):14.

Provan, Keith G. "Board Power and Organizational Effectiveness Among Human Service Agencies." *Academy of Management Journal* 23(June 1980):221-36.

Reiss, Albert J., Jr.; Duncan, Otis Dudley; Hatt, Paul K.; and North, Cecil C. *Occupations and Social Status.* New York: The Free Press of Glenco, Inc., 1961.

Religious Observance by Muslim Employees: A Framework for Discussion. London: Commission for Radical Equality, March 1980.

Rodgers, Daniel T. "'Work Ethic' More a Matter of Need than Desire to Work." *Sunday Herald-Times,* Bloomington, Indiana (11 October 1981):12-13.

Roll, Eric. *A History of Economic Thought.* Boston: Faber & Faber Ltd., 1978.

Roof, Wade Clark. "White American Socioreligious Groups and Work Values." *Electricity* 7(June 1980):214-24.

Rose, Jeffrey, and Ignatieff, Michael, eds. *Religion and International Affairs.* Toronto: House of Auansi Press, 1968.

Rotwein, Eugene, ed. *David Hume: Writings on Economics.* Madison, WI: The University of Wisconsin Press, 1970.

Sanders, Sol. W. "Iran's Victory Will Tip a Fragile Balance." *Business Week* (22 March 1982):54.

_____. "The Moderate Who May Be the Next Mideast Target." *Business Week* (26 October 1981):99.

Sanders, Thomas G. *The Catholic Church in Brazil's Political Transition.* Hanover, NH: American Universities Field Staff, 1980 (No. 48, TGS-3-'80).

_____. *Food Policy Decision-Making in Colombia.* Hanover, NH: American Universities Field Staff, 1980 (No. 50, TGS-4-'80).

Schall, James V. "American Catholics and the American Productive System." Paper presented at the Summer 1981 American Enterprise Institute, Washington, DC, 7-9 July 1981.

Schiffman, Leon G., Dillon, William R., and Ngumah, Festus E. "The Influence of Subcultural and Personality Factors on Consumer Acculturation." *Journal of International Business Studies* 12(Fall 1981):137-43.

Schoorman, F. David, Bazerman, Max H., and Atkin, Robert S. "Interlocking Directorates: A Strategy for Reducing Environmental Uncertainty." *Academy of Management Review* 6(April 1981):243-51.

Schumpeter, Joseph A. *Capitalism, Socialism, and Democracy.* New York: Harper and Brothers, Publishers, 1947.

_____. *History of Economic Analysis.* London: George Allen & Unwin, Ltd., 1967.

Scott, William G., Mitchell, Terence R., and Birnbaum, Philip H. *Organization Theory: A Structural and Behavioral Analysis.* Homewood, IL: Richard D. Irwin, Inc., 1981.

Selznick, Philip. *TVA and the Grass Roots: A Study in the Sociology of Formal Organization.* New York: Harper & Row, Publishers, 1966.

Silvert, Kalman H. and Reissman, Leonard. *Education, Class, and Nation: The Experiences of Chile and Venezuela.* New York: Elsevier Scientific Publishing Company, 1976.

"Sisters of the Third World." *Newsweek* (22 December 1980):75.

Smith, Adam. *The Wealth of Nations.* Vols. 1-3, edited by Andrew Skinner. New York: Penguin Books, 1978.

Smith, Wilfred Cantwell. *Islam in Modern History.* New York: Mentor Books, 1957.

Soto, Antonio R. "Ethnic Minorities Within a Religious Institution: The Case of the Chicano and the Church in California." Paper presented at the 7th Annual Conference on Ethnic and Minority Studies, LaCrosse, WI, 2-5 May 1979.

Staw, Barry M., and Szwajkowski, Eugene. "The Scarcity-Munificence Component of Organizational Environments and the Commission of Illegal Acts." *Administrative Science Quarterly* 20(September 1975):345-54.

Steiner, George A. "Contingency Theories of Strategy and Strategic Management." In *Strategic Management: A New View of Business Policy and Planning,* edited by Dan E. Schendel and Charles W. Hofer. Boston: Little, Brown and Company, 1979.

Tawney, R.H. *Religion and the Rise of Capitalism.* New York: Harcourt, Brace and Company, Inc., 1926.

Terpstra, Vern. *The Cultural Environment of International Business.* Cincinnati, OH: South-Western Publishing Co., 1978.

Terreberry, Shirley. "The Evolution of Organization Environments." In *Contemporary Sociological Theory,* edited by Fred E. Katz. New York: Random House Publishers, 1971.

Thompson, James D., ed. *Approaches to Organizational Design.* Pittsburgh Press, 1966.

———. *Organizations in Action.* New York: McGraw Hill, 1967.

———, and McEwen, William J. "Organizational Goals and Environment: Goal Setting as an Interaction Process." In *Readings in Organization Theory: Open Systems Approaches,* edited by John G. Maurer. New York: Random House, 1971.

Thorkelson, W.L. "Judge Calls on Corporations to Repent." *Lutheran* 20(6 January 1982):21.

Tonsor, Stephen J. "The Medieval Model of Social Reconstruction and the 19th and 20th Century Reality." Paper presented at the Summer 1981 American Enterprise Institute Workshop, Washington, DC, 7-9 July 1981.

Topel, L. John. *The Way to Peace.* New York: Maryknoll, 1979.

Treacy, Gerald C., ed. *Five Great Encyclicals.* New York: The Paulist Press, 1953.

Trexler, Edgar R. "1984: 'Year of Tension' in Religion." *Lutheran* 23(2 January 1985):20.

Ulman, Neil. "Church and Labor Seek 'Just Society' in Brazil as Key Elections Near." *Wall Street Journal* (21 September 1982):1, 22.

United Nations Department of Public Information. *Pope John Paul II at the United Nations.* New York: United Nations Publication, 1980.

U.S. Congress. Senate. Subcommittee on Reports, Accounting and Management of the Committee on Governmental Affairs. *Interlocking Directorates Among the Major U.S. Corporations.* 95th Congress, 2nd session, January 1978.

U.S. Department of Commerce, Bureau of the Census. United States Census of Population: 1960. Vol. 1, *Characteristics of the Population.* Part 16, Indiana. Washington, DC.

———. United States Census of Population: 1970. Vol. 1, *Characteristics of the Population.* Part 16, Indiana. Washington, DC.

Viner, Jacob. *Religious Thought and Economic Society,* edited by Jacques Melitz and Donald Winch, Durham, NC: Duke University Press, 1978.

Weber, Alfred. *History of Philosophy,* translated by Frank Thilly. New York: Charles Scribner's Sons, 1925.

Weber, Max. *The Protestant Ethic and the Spirit of Capitalism.* New York: Charles Scribner's Sons, 1958.

Weick, Karl E. *The Social Psychology of Organizing.* Reading, MA: Addison-Wesley Publishing Co., 1969.

Wilson, George W., ed. *Classics of Economic Theory.* Bloomington, IN: Indiana University Press, 1964.

———. "The Economics of Just Price." *History of Political Economy* (Spring 1975):56-74.

Wuthnow, Robert, ed. *The Religious Dimension: New Directions in Quantitative Research.* New York: Academic Press, 1979.

Yuchtman E. and Seashore, S. "A Systems Resource Approach to Organizational Effect." *American Sociological Review* 32(December 1967):891-903.

Zald, M.N. "The Power and Function of Boards of Directors: A Theoretical Synthesis." *American Journal of Sociology* 75(July 1969):97-111.

_____. "Urban Differentiation, Characteristics of Boards of Directors and Organizational Effectiveness." *American Journal of Sociology* 73(November 1967):261-72.

Index